Praise for *Living the Sabbath*

"In our hot-and-now commodity culture, in which even religion is often seen as just another thing to be consumed, *Living the Sabbath* is a clarion call to retrieve the wisdom of the biblical understanding of Sabbath. Clearly and engagingly written, free of scholarly clutter, and brim full of much practical insight on how to live with joy and delight, Norman Wirzba's book is a welcome and timely addition to the Christian Practice of Everyday Life series. This book deserves a wide readership."

—Steven Bouma-Prediger, Hope College

"Norman Wirzba's *Living the Sabbath* takes us beyond the usual depictions of Sabbath as individual retreat into the practices of Sabbath that engage the fullness of our lives. He explores what it means to live out of a sense of Sabbath in family and community relationships, work and social commitments, and in the theological expressions of 'delight in the goodness of God.' Here is a text for living simply and in the continuing transformation of our lives by God's grace."

—Malcolm Lyle Warford, Lexington Theological Seminary

"This book reads so well that you're tempted to speed through it. But don't. Enjoy it with a glass of iced tea; sit in your rocking chair on the porch and savor it, read slowly, let it sink in. Turn off the television, stay away from the mall, have a conversation with your neighbors, eat home-grown tomatoes. Practice it while you read it. Learn to do Sabbath. Take delight."

—Kyle Childress, pastor of Austin Heights Baptist Church,
Nacogdoches, Texas

Living
the Sabbath

The Christian Practice
of Everyday Life

David S. Cunningham
and William T. Cavanaugh, series editors

This series seeks to present specifically Christian perspectives on some of the most prevalent contemporary practices of everyday life. It is intended for a broad audience—including clergy, interested laypeople, and students. The books in this series are motivated by the conviction that, in the contemporary context, Christians must actively demonstrate that their allegiance to the God of Jesus Christ always takes priority over secular structures that compete for our loyalty—including the state, the market, race, class, gender, and other functional idolatries. The books in this series will examine these competing allegiances as they play themselves out in particular day-to-day practices, and will provide concrete descriptions of how the Christian faith might play a more formative role in our everyday lives.

The Christian Practice of Everyday Life series is an initiative of The Ekklesia Project, an ecumenical gathering of pastors, theologians, and lay leaders committed to helping the church recall its status as the distinctive, real-world community dedicated to the priorities and practices of Jesus Christ and to the inbreaking Kingdom of God. (For more information on The Ekklesia Project, see <www.ekklesiaproject.org>.)

Living the Sabbath

Discovering the Rhythms of Rest and Delight

THE CHRISTIAN PRACTICE OF EVERYDAY LIFE Series

Norman Wirzba

BrazosPress
a division of Baker Publishing Group
Grand Rapids, Michigan

Published by Brazos Press
a division of Baker Publishing Group
P.O. Box 6287, Grand Rapids, MI 49516-6287
www.brazospress.com

Printed in the United States of America

Library of Congress Cataloging-in-Publication Data
Wirzba, Norman.
    Living the Sabbath : discovering the rhythms of rest and delight / Norman Wirzba.
        p.   cm. — (The Christian practice of everyday life)
    Includes bibliographical references.
    ISBN 10: 1-58743-165-3 (pbk.)
    ISBN 978-1-58743-165-4 (pbk.)
    1. Rest—Religious aspects—Christianity. 2. Sabbath. I. Title. II. Series.
BV4597.55.W57 2006
263′.1—dc22   2006010011

For Gretchen

"Unto my Mind again repair:
Which makes my Life a Circle of Delights . . ."

Contents

Foreword

■ We are living at the climax of industrialism. The "cheap" fossil fuels, on which our world has grown dependent, are now becoming expensive in money and in lives. The industrial era at climax, in the panic of long-anticipated decline, has imposed on us all its ideals of ceaseless pandemonium. The industrial economy, by definition, must never rest. Rest would deprive us of light, heat, food, water, and everything else we need or think we need. The economic impulse of industrial life (to stretch a term) is limitless. Whatever we have, in whatever quantity, is not enough. There is no such thing as enough. Our bellies and our wallets must become oceanic, and still they will not be full. Six workdays in a week are not enough. We need a seventh. We need an eighth. In the industrial world, at climax, one family cannot or will not support itself by one job. We need a job for the day and one for the night. Thank God for the moon! We cannot stop to eat. Thank God for cars! We dine as we drive over another paved farm. Everybody is weary, and there is no rest.

To rest, we are persuaded, we must "get away." But getting away involves us in the haste, speed, and noise, the auxiliary pandemonium, of escape. There is, by the prevailing definition, escape, but there is no escape from escape. Or there is none unless we adopt the paradoxical and radical expedient of just stopping.

Just stopping is the opportune subject of this book. The thought of just stopping is not new and it is not simple. In biblical tradition, it is one of the oldest thoughts. Humans, one must suppose, thought of stopping soon after they had thought of whatever first made them tired. But biblical tradition elevates just stopping above physiology necessity, makes it a requirement, makes it an observance of the greatest dignity and mystery, and assigns it a day. The day is named Sabbath. On that day people are to come to rest, just stop, and not merely because they are tired; they are to do so in commemoration of the seventh day, the day on which, after the six days of creation, God rested.

He was not able to rest until the seventh day because the creation was not completed until the end of the sixth day. The world, once it was made, was not complete in the sense that it was "done" or "finished." It was complete because it was whole. Its maker had so filled it with living creatures so invested with his spirit and breath that it could keep on working, it could live on its own, while he rested. It was an active and ongoing wholeness. It was a wholeness that could adapt and change; it could "evolve," as you may say if you wish. That too.

And so the humans who "remember the Sabbath day" do so not only to rest, but also to honor the rest of the seventh day, which perfected the work of the six days. This rest is made possible by the capability of the creation, once made whole, to continue indefinitely on the basis of its originating principles and its culminating goodness. The creation is a living work in which every creature must participate, by its own nature and by the nature of the world. We humans, by *our* particular nature, must participate for better or worse, and this is our choice to make. Will we choose to participate by working in accordance with the world's originating principles, in recognition of its inherent goodness and its maker's approval of it, in gratitude for our membership in it, or will we participate by destroying it in accordance with our always tottering, never resting self-justifications and selfish desires?

The requirement of Sabbath observance invites us to stop. It invites us to rest. It asks us to notice that while we rest the world continues without our help. It invites us to find delight in the world's beauty and abundance. (Thank God for cheap recreation!) Now, in our pandemonium, it may be asking us also to consider that if we choose not to honor it and care well for it, the world will continue in our absence.

The life of this world is by no means simple or comprehensible to us humans. It involves darkness and suffering; it confronts us daily with mystery and our ignorance. But the idea of the Sabbath passes through it as a vein of light, reminding us of the inherent sanctity of the world and our life, and of the transformative sanity of admiration, gratitude, and care. Norman Wirzba's book asks what kind of human life it takes to include the Sabbath. It is high time somebody asked. As this book shows, what is implied is a set of answers dangerous to ignore.

Wendell Berry

Preface

■ There is an ancient rabbinic tradition that says if we learn to celebrate the Sabbath properly and fully even once, the Messiah will come. This is a striking view because it suggests that Sabbath observance is the fulfillment or perfection of a religious life that is harmoniously tuned to the life-giving and life-promoting ways of God. Without the Sabbath, in other words, faith, but also life itself, is in peril of losing its most basic and comprehensive orientation and purpose. Just as God's *shabbat* completes the creation of the universe—by demonstrating that the proper response to the gifts of life is celebration and delight—so too should our Sabbaths be the culmination of habits and days that express gratitude for and joy in the manifold blessings of God.

It makes sense, therefore, to think of Sabbath observance as one of our most honest and practical indicators of authentic religious faith. The extent and depth of our Sabbath commitment is the measure of how far we have progressed in our discipleship and friendship with God. Our Sabbath commitment bears witness to whether or not we have brought our habits and priorities in line with the ways and intentions of God. When we fail to observe the Sabbath we miss out on the chance to experience creation and each other as God desires it. We forfeit the opportunity to live our days in the modes of care, celebration, and delight—all marks of the first Sabbath day.

It is dangerous, of course, to presume to speak for "the ways and intentions of God," because we easily forget or deny that our speaking is often motivated by arrogance, fear, or fancy. In the end, God's ways with the world, indeed God creating a world at all, confront us with mysteries that elude our best efforts to comprehend. As fallible and finite creatures the best that we can do is move with caution and humility, trusting that our efforts to align our lives with God's intentions are throughout informed and shaped by God's self-revelation to us. In this book I suggest that Sabbath teaching contains an inner logic that helps us make some theological and practical sense of God's revelation. When understood in its proper depth and breadth, the Sabbath not only situates us within the orders of creation, and thus within the larger drama of God's redeeming love, but also opens new paths as we journey toward justice, peace, and joy.

The central significance of the Sabbath, though well understood (if not always faithfully observed) by the ancient Israelites, has mostly been lost to us. In part this is because frantic and competing schedules make it much more difficult to keep a Sabbath focus, particularly if by Sabbath observance we understand communal rest one full day in the week. Many of us, whether we be pastors, caregivers, store managers, medical staff, teachers, farmers, emergency service personnel, or athletes, do not have the time at all or do not have it when we need it: some of us are required to work on the formal day of the Sabbath or feel we need to use the day to catch up on the myriad tasks we failed to complete during the course of the week. A "free day" or "day off" constitutes a luxury many of us simply cannot imagine, let alone afford. Who will do the laundry and the grocery shopping, or prepare the lesson plan and the meeting's agenda? Moreover, given the pluralistic, multiethnic character of global cultures, we can no longer assume a shared social understanding or commonality of purpose that would grant to communities as a whole the time and place to celebrate a Sabbath. Does this mean we are doomed?

This book lays out the case for Sabbath observance that does not depend on the cultural sanction of complete rest for one day of the week. Though such a practice is still and always will be a desirable goal, many of us need additional suggestions for daily practices—alternative rituals—that can move us into the heart of the Sabbath. The question for us is whether in doing so we can approximate a Sabbath sensibility that realizes many of its central aims. Can we envision contemporary avenues for the practices of delight, thanksgiving, and praise—quintessential indicators that we are at rest—that will transform our daily and weekly habits? This book argues that we can, but if we are to accomplish this we must expand the range of Sabbath reference so that all our days and activities fall within its orbit. I do not want to minimize the importance of setting aside one day of the week for special religious observance. Indeed, in many instances the frantic and frenetic pace of our activities simply needs to come to a stop. But I also want us to appreciate that the Sabbath is not confined to one day. Sabbath observance has the potential to reform and redirect all our ways of living. It should be the source and goal that inspires and nourishes the best of everything we do.

If we are to live the Sabbath in this more expansive way, we need to think differently about what it means. The Sabbath is not simply about taking a break from our busy routines. It should not be reduced to a "time of rest" understood as inactivity, because this formulation overlooks the rich potential within Sabbath teaching to transform a complete life. This book therefore devotes several chapters to an exploration of the Sabbath's rich meanings, and then considers why it is difficult to appreciate and realize Sabbath goals within our personal and communal lives. As I will argue, the key to Sabbath observance is that we participate regularly in the delight that marked God's own response to a creation wonderfully made.

In the second part of the book I develop several chapters on how to make Sabbath delight real in the various dimensions of daily life: at work, in the home, in our economies and schools, in our care of creation, and in the church. Sabbath teaching has the potential to elevate all our practices so that they bring honor to God and delight to the world. When we become a Sabbath people, we give one of the most compelling witnesses to the world that we worship a God who desires our collective joy and good. We give concrete expression to an authentic faith that is working to deflate the anxious and destructive pride that supposes we have to "do it all" by ourselves and through our own effort. Our faith replaces such selfish ambition with a holy desire that God's life-building and life-affirming ways become more manifest through us. We also become participants in God's redemptive purposes for the whole world by attending to and addressing the pain and injustice that currently deny God's desire that all of creation be well and at peace. In short, Sabbath observance has the potential to release the depth and meaning of God's many blessings at work within creation and in all of our doings.

I am not an "expert" in Sabbath observance. Like many others, I struggle to practice delight and to ponder and properly imitate the goodness of God. Indeed, much of what I have learned about the rich meaning of the Sabbath has been as a witness to personal failure. I take comfort, as should you the reader, in the fact that the ancient Israelites developed this teaching over many generations and through much trial and error. What sustains us in our Sabbath journey is the companionship and support of fellow travelers who inspire us to be more faithful and who bear witness to the excellence and loveliness of the ways of delight. For their gifts of friendship and help, I would like to thank Gretchen Ziegenhals, Stanley Hauerwas, Kyle Childress, Rodney Clapp, Rebecca Cooper, and Wendell Berry, who read sections or the whole of this manuscript in earlier versions, making valuable suggestions for improvement. I would especially like to thank Wendell Berry for writing a foreword to this book. Their kindness and insight have made this a better book. No doubt it would have been even better had I heeded all of their suggestions. To them I offer heartfelt thanks.

Part 1

Setting a Sabbath Context

1

Losing Our Way

■ By most accounts, the average North American today enjoys one of the highest standards of living humanity has ever known. In fact, many of us lead comfortable and luxurious lives that heretofore would have been unimaginable to, let alone the envy of, kings and queens. Given our much trumpeted prosperity and success, we should wonder why we don't really seem to *enjoy* our lives very much. For all that we have achieved, our lives, as viewed in their day-to-day ordinariness, do not appear measurably happier. Moreover, the social and ecological costs associated with our success—habitat destruction and family and community deterioration—are becoming increasingly difficult to ignore.

Many of us submit to daily schedules that keep us moving at a soul-blistering, exhaustion-inducing pace, and we agree to ever-lengthening to-do lists that invariably leave us stretched or stressed to the breaking point. To be sure, we have a lot to show for our efforts in the extensive résumés we compile and in the mountains of stuff we store in our basements, garages, and off-site self-storage lockers (now a multibillion-dollar industry). But despite our many career accomplishments and consumer acquisitions, we are not satisfied or at peace. We are forever hounded by the worry that we do not yet have quite enough, or that what we have is not the latest, fastest, or most fashionable best, and the fear that we will be perceived as slackers.

To help us through this chaotic, soul-unsatisfying chaos, we frequently turn to pharmaceutical enhancers and stimulants—Prozac, Viagra, Prilosec (the "Purple Pill"), Lipitor, Ambien—to keep us going through our paces. In doing so we simply ignore or override the natural bodily signs—exhaustion, hypertension, obesity, anxiety, insomnia—that would otherwise alert us to the fact that something is terribly wrong with the way we are conducting our lives. Is this not a strategy in which we will all finally turn out to be losers?

The frantic, fragmenting, multitasking character of contemporary living has made it likely that many of us will simply evade, or fail to consider with much seriousness or depth, life's most basic and profound questions: What is all our living finally for? Why do we commit to so much? Why do we devote ourselves to the tasks or priorities that we do? Will we know when we have achieved or acquired enough? What purpose does our striving serve? While these questions point to the basic ingredients of any recipe for a decent human life, they are also vital to the life of faith, for in pondering them we not only become clearer about our ultimate allegiances but also gain insight into who we understand ourselves to be. In answering them we get a clearer picture of how closely our intentions and our living line up with the purposes of God. Do we truly believe ourselves to be children of God and members of creation, and thus able to trust in God's beneficent care and provision?

A Sabbath Bearing

Though we don't often think of it this way, biblical teaching on the Sabbath takes us to the heart of this essential questioning. Rather than being simply a "break" from frenetic, self-obsessed ways of living, the Sabbath is a discipline and practice in which we ask, consider, and answer the questions that will lead us into a complete and joyful life. As such, the Sabbath is a teaching that has the potential to redirect and transform all our existence, bringing it into more faithful alignment with God's life-building and life-strengthening ways. Sabbath life is a truly human life—abundant life, life at its best—because it is founded in God's overarching design for all places (Sabbath celebration completes the creation of the universe) and all times (Sabbath worship is the week's fulfillment and inspiration). Though the Sabbath does not promise a life without pain and suffering, its observance does offer the practical context through which our collective hurt can be addressed (if not always answered).

Sabbath teaching best equips us to think about the ultimate bearing or direction of human life. It gives us a glimpse and a taste of the all-encompassing divine context in terms of which we can formulate and evaluate our life plan. Better than anything else, it helps us appreciate and understand what all our living is finally for. Put simply, Sabbath discipline introduces us to God's own ways of joy and delight. In the invitation that follows from it, we are given the opportunity to share in the divine life of love and peace.

Psalm 92, the Bible's own "Song for the Sabbath Day," lets us know immediately that a Sabbath way of living stands in marked contrast to our current stressful, exhausting, death-wielding ways. According to the psalmist, Sabbath observance is above all infused with thanksgiving and praise. Insofar as our practical living grows out of a grateful disposition, a sense that the gifts of God to us far exceed what we can comprehend or expect, we give concrete witness to the world of a God whose generosity and care simply know no bounds. When our work and our play, our exertion and our rest flow seamlessly from this deep desire to give thanks to God, the totality of our living—cooking, eating, cleaning, preaching, teaching, parenting, building, repairing, healing, creating—becomes one sustained and ever-expanding act of worship.

> It is good to give thanks to the LORD,
>   to sing praises to your name, O Most High;
> to declare your steadfast love in the morning,
>   and your faithfulness by night,
> to the music of the lute and the harp,
>   to the melody of the lyre.

According to the psalmist, our offerings of thanksgiving and praise are not a forced or commanded response. When they are at their most authentic pitch, they follow spontaneously and naturally from a life that is attentive and responsive to God's grandeur and goodness everywhere on display.

> For you, O LORD, have made me glad by your work;
>   at the works of your hands I sing for joy.
>
> How great are your works, O LORD!
>   Your thoughts are very deep!

The work of God's hand, the whole panorama of creation—flowers, bees, photosynthesis, earthworms, rain, humus, chickens, sheep, babies, families, and friendships—testifies to God who cares intimately and deeply about the world and desires that it be beautiful and at peace. The psalmist believes that those who do not see this beauty and feel inwardly the marks of divine care are simply fools. They are guilty of a fundamental blindness and insensitivity, an inability to see the world for what it really is: the concrete manifestation of God's incomparable *hesed*, God's covenantal and creative love for the whole world. Being ignorant fools, they are likely to become wicked by destroying or spoiling the good gifts of God that are the nurturing root of our being and the inexhaustible source of our joy. The psalmist does not mince words:

> The dullard cannot know,
>   the stupid cannot understand this:
> though the wicked sprout like grass
>   and all evildoers flourish,
> they are doomed to destruction forever,
>   but you, O LORD, are on high forever.
> For your enemies, O LORD,
>   for your enemies shall perish;
>   all evildoers shall be scattered. (92:1–9)

It is not a comforting exercise to contemplate whether we are among the dullards and the stupid, or whether our aggressive and anxious patterns of living place us among the enemies of God. But we need to consider this as a real possibility. Why? Because it is surprisingly easy to be dishonest about our piety. We have to admit the possibility that we have overestimated our devotion, particularly when we note the overwhelming evidence of human destruction and despoliation of communities and creation *in the midst of our religiously informed culture*. Though we may speak words of praise and thanks, does our living concretely manifest the deep gladness and appreciation, the celebration and respect the psalmist models, and thus render our speaking true?

I begin to wonder why my days are not given over to more joyful and harmonious singing, following directly and spontaneously from the knowledge that I am at peace with the world around me. If I am honest with myself, I acknowledge a serious lack of readiness and desire to cherish the many gifts of creation that sustain and inspire me. I do not nearly enough devote myself to the caretaking and celebration of all God's bewildering array of blessing. The result, more often than not, is self-pain and pain to those around me. Collectively, our anxious obsessions prevent us from adequately considering and enjoying the convivial life God so much wants for us.

Psalm 92 not only stands as an indictment against today's culture of exhaustion and destruction. It also presents us with a positive vision of the Sabbath that takes us far beyond all notions of Sabbath observance as a mere reprieve from six days of frantic exertion. Sabbath practice is the focus and culmination of a life that is daily and practically devoted to honoring God, the source of all our delight and the provider of every good and perfect gift, and to sharing in God's own creative delight. We do not wait for one specified day of the week to offer our thanksgiving and praise, even if one day is set apart to shed a critical and corrective light on all our other days. The goal is rather to arrange our schedules and direct our choices so that they manifest *at all times* a deep appreciation for the diverse and costly ways of God's grace. That we cultivate such sensitivity and understanding in each other is absolutely essential if we are not to become wicked fools, the spoilers of grace who take the *hesed* of God for granted. The seriousness of our failing to adopt a Sabbath way of life comes through clearly in the rabbinic view that on the day of judgment we will need to give an account for all the times we did not sufficiently or properly celebrate the gifts of God's creation.

If the psalmist is right, then the test of whether we have genuinely practiced the Sabbath will come in the middle of our working week, as we are building, teaching, healing, cooking, rather than the formal (and sometimes merely formulaic) setting of a "worship service." We need to learn to evaluate our mundane, daily, practical activities and aspirations in light of the Sabbath goals of praise and thanksgiving to God. Does our obsession with personal accomplishment, and the anxious insecurity it often tries to mask, deny God's unfailing affirmation of and care for us? Does our planning for financial control and security (as manifested in countless daily tasks) practically contradict our verbal expressions of faith and hope in the goodness and generosity of God? In these diverse times and places—our investment portfolios, career aspirations, housing preferences, consumer habits, extracurricular activities—a more honest reckoning of our piety will become possible. Moreover, as we begin to cast a Sabbath light on the whole sweep of our activities and routines by looking for occasions to be thankful and to celebrate, we may yet catch glimpses of God's sustaining presence and abiding goodness in places we never thought possible.

That the Sabbath should assume such importance in the life of faith will likely sound strange to many of us, because we have grown used to thinking of Sabbath observance as an add-on to the end of a busy week. Sabbath is the time for us to relax and let down our guard, to pause from the often anxious and competitive patterns of daily life. This is not what the Jews, those who first gave us the teaching about Sabbath, thought. In their view, Sabbath observance is what we work *toward*. As our most important and all-encompassing goal, it frames and contextualizes our planning, much as the desire to achieve a specific objective—a championship, a masterful performance, an exquisite meal or party—will require that we take the proper steps *all along the way*. Sabbath frames our entire life, helping us set priorities and determine which of our activities and aspirations bring honor to God.

So what is at stake in Sabbath observance is not simply that we manage to pause and refuel enough to continue on in our frantic and sometimes destructive ways. The real issue is whether we can learn to see, and then welcome, the divine presence wherever we are. Can we link up as servants of God's covenantal love and see in that service our unending joy? Doing this, we will learn to realign all of our activities so that they better manifest a life of gratitude and praise. If we can do this truly, without the anxiety, worry, fear, competitiveness, and aggression that otherwise punctuate our life's patterns, then we will have caught a glimpse of heaven, a taste of God's own delight in a created order beautifully and finely made. Indeed, as Abraham Joshua Heschel once observed, "Unless one learns how to relish the taste of Sabbath while still in this world, unless one is initiated in the appreciation of eternal life, one will be unable to enjoy the taste of eternity in the world to come."[1] We are simply naive if we think that having wasted or squandered the many good gifts of this creation, we will not do the same with the gifts of heaven. Sabbath practice, on this view, is a sort of training ground for the life of eternity, a preparation for the full reception and welcome of the presence of God.

Eating as a Sabbath Witness

In light of the Sabbath's practical and far-reaching significance, an obvious question is, How are we doing? Does our culture reflect a Sabbath sensibility that has made gratitude and praise to God its foremost concern? Are our church communities—not merely our church services—daily marked by forms of celebration that mirror God's own delight in the works of creation? To answer these questions with the greatest honesty and precision possible, we will need to consider carefully the condition and health of all members of creation—friends and family members, but also the disenfranchised, the sick and feeble, the soil on which we walk, the air we breathe, the water we drink, the natural organisms that make up our biological neighborhood, and the geophysical processes that sustain us all—within our control or influence. Does our engagement with them indicate that we are grateful to God for them and appreciate them as a blessing to us? Do we honor God in our treatment of them, acknowledging that without them our lives would be impoverished or severely impaired? If we are truly thankful for the gifts of God, these same gifts will be cherished and cared for. If they are not well cared for, we will have to assume that gratitude and praise have been overcome by our anxieties, fears, obsessions, insensitivities, and arrogance.

I suggest that eating habits reflect one of our more profound, even if mundane, paths into the full awareness of God's care and concern. When we eat, we ingest God's life-sustaining gifts. At mealtimes and snack times we experience the fresh, sweet, tasty, diverse generosity of God. In the handling and consuming of the bodies of creation we come into direct contact with the love of God, and so experience again and again the divine, hospitable love that brought all creation into being. Herbert McCabe has suggested that the generosity evident in our eating, when followed through thoughtfully enough, brings us (much like Thomas Aquinas's famous "five ways" for demonstrating the existence of God) to an appreciation of the mysterious and deep source of life we call God. "When we say grace we acknowledge our meal as an expression of God's love for us, as communication from God, as word from God." When our eating is informed by God's love and care, we participate in the new humanity of God made possible by Jesus Christ, who is called our true food and drink. "By saying grace, by saying thanks, we recognize this meal [the Eucharist], this medium of human unity as gift of the Father, as ordered to the greater kind of unity he is to give us in Christ."[2] Eating, we can now see, is one of the most fundamental ways we know for communicating our life together as a gift gratefully received and cherished.

The current state of food production, particularly meat production, gives us one of the clearest indicators that we have forsaken a Sabbath way of life and refused to order our economic choices according to Sabbath priorities.[3] Though few of us have much direct involvement in the raising of food, we all eat and thus daily enact our interdependencies with the whole spectrum of God's creation. Thus eating, whether we recognize it or not, takes us to the heart of what a culture is about and what it sees as valuable and important. To think about Italy or Mexico or China as a culture, for example, is automatically to think about its people's food and their habits of food preparation and consumption. Does the character of our culture's current food production, distribution, and consumption show forth gratitude and praise?

Many of us are not in a good position to answer this question because we are ignorant about where food comes from and under what conditions it is produced. When we remember that for most of our history the great majority of people were directly or indirectly involved with the growth, preparation, and storage of food, the contrast is sharp. Given the insularity and artificiality of suburban life, we eat with unprecedented ignorance. Food is something we buy at a store, neatly packaged, at a relatively cheap price. Seeing, then smelling and tasting, its attractiveness and abundance, we are lulled into assuming that our food is responsibly produced. Our ignorance and our naiveté prevent us from inquiring beyond the slick packaging our food comes in.

If we were to examine further, we would quickly discover that our food industry bears all the marks of an anti-Sabbath mentality: sacrilege and ingratitude, obsessive control and profiteering, insensitivity and destruction. Today's food industry has reduced the gifts of God to "products" or "commodities" that are manufactured and processed to maximize stockholder values. Much of our production of cereals and vegetables is premised on the use of massive amounts of fertilizers and pesticides—toxins and poisons that leach into our groundwater and runoff systems and finally contribute to large "dead zones" in our bays and oceans—and unsustainable rates of soil erosion and water depletion. Further, the cheap price and relative abundance of our current grain supply depend heavily on fossil fuel and the increasing exhaustion and gradual elimination of our soil base. The (misnamed) Green Revolution would not have been possible, nor can it be maintained, without cheap oil.

The ungrateful and deathly character of our food industry is even more pronounced in the meat production sector. Though our children's picture books and many advertisements and commercials suggest that animal livestock are raised on family farms in which chickens, geese, pigs, sheep, and cattle have freedom to roam and to be, this is not the case. Of the ten billion animals slaughtered in the United States last year, the overwhelming majority were raised in massive confinement operations that gave them little room to move and little access to fresh air and sunlight. Pigs, born to root and roam as they socialize and look for grubs, are often locked in stalls that do not provide enough room for them even to turn around. Chickens are crammed, eight at a time, into wire crates no bigger than the drawer of a filing cabinet. These crates are stacked on top of each other in darkness, which means that chickens higher up defecate on those below. Illness and anxiety run rampant, and so heavy uses of antibiotics are required to keep the fowl healthy enough till slaughter. Being in wire cages, chickens often lose feathers, develop sore feet, or get hung up on stray wires that render them immobile or perpetually uncomfortable. Since there are tens of thousands of chickens in each "barn," many of the dead simply stay in their crates until it is time for the living to be removed.

The human beings who work in these confinement operations find the conditions deplorable and cruel and so often do not last long in that employment. Agricultural work has some of the highest turnover rates and some of the lowest wages. No creature, whether worker or victim, should be compelled to live like this. How does the living of animals directly under our control honor God or reflect gratitude for them?

When factory-farmed animals leave confinement, their condition does not much improve. In some cases it worsens. Due to the deregulation of the slaughterhouse industry and the desire to maximize profits, animals enter what can be called a factory disassembly line. Rather than being killed in humane fashion, and as kosher methods of slaughter recommend, quickly and with as little stress and pain as possible, animals may be boiled, skinned, or dismembered while still alive. The speed of the "line" or "rail" that carries the animal through various stages of the butchering process is simply too fast for workers to exercise the requisite care and attention. Besides being a torment to animals, the work is very dangerous to workers, who have disproportionately high injury rates. Safety regulations are not adequately enforced, and workers are prevented from banding together to lobby for better conditions. The misery of animals is thus compounded by the misery of workers who find no occasion for Sabbath delight or praise in their work.

Not enough people acknowledge or understand this dark side to the slick packaging and cheap pricing of our meat products. Indeed, it is quite likely that if we saw the meat industry up close (something the industry has worked hard to prevent), our eating habits and preferences would change dramatically. The issue, however, is not simply whether we should become vegetarians, particularly when we remember that many of our grain and vegetable crops are also produced in a destructive and unsustainable manner. The real issue is whether we can learn to grow food and eat in a way that reflects thanksgiving and praise to God.

My grandfather, I believe, understood what this meant. As a small farmer, he raised a variety of animals for sale and for food. His treatment of them was uniformly attentive and kind. In fact, his gentle demeanor would rarely turn to anger and frustration—and then usually only in response to another's (my) mistreatment of them. In his view, every animal was a gift from God that merited our respect and care. Nowhere was this more apparent than in his treatment of our chickens.

In the summer he would regularly give up his afternoon rest period to find an especially lush, sweet patch of grass to cut as a treat for the chickens. After gathering the grass in a bucket, he would walk to the chicken coop with an air of sheer delight, for without fail the chickens would run to greet him and gobble down the fresh blades of grass. I would swear the chickens had smiles on their faces as they came running! Nothing made my grandfather happier than seeing the chickens so much enjoy his little offering.

From an economic standpoint, what he did was unnecessary, even foolish, because it took him away from what others would have considered to be his "important" work. Our chickens had plenty to eat and could roam the farmyard at will. They could get their own grass if they wanted it. I am convinced, however, that this little labor meant so much to him because it enacted a ritual of mutual delight. In these moments my grandfather recalled God's proclamation of the goodness of the whole creation. He saw his chickens as a splendid gift from God that merited his attention, care, and celebration. His work was an act of worship, since it confirmed and contributed to the goodness that was already there. It also resulted in a more thankful life. When my grandfather sat down to a chicken dinner, as he often did, he ate with a realistic and palpable sense of the goodness and the costliness of creation—after all, these chickens had died so that he could eat. Their death could not be taken lightly, nor could their living. And so their very being demanded our respect and care. His eating was a sacramental eating, because it affirmed the grace and beneficence of God made concrete in the midst of his living. It was a Sabbath eating, permeated by his thanksgiving and praise to God.

It All Turns on Praise

As Ellen Davis has reminded us, "Praise does more for *us* than it does for God." The reason we worship is not so that God will be impressed with us. It is rather that we will become less sentimental, less self-absorbed, and more realistic about the life God has given. The activity of praise serves the most important function of helping us correct and train our desires: "we praise God in order to see the world as God does."[4] And so when the psalmist counsels us to praise God, he is interested in how this activity transforms us and effects a new and more honest relationship to the world. When we praise God, we commit ourselves to the world as it came forth and continues to be sustained by God's loving hands.

What does God want for the whole creation? If we are honest, we can readily see how that question has been usurped by another: what do *we* want from the world? As we adopt a posture of praise, however, our daily lives will be reordered so that the priorities of God take precedence. First among these priorities is that the well-being of all creation, ourselves included, be secured and celebrated. If we are serious about praising God with our lives and not just our words, we will learn to act differently, for it is in our mundane daily living that we show most honestly what we think all life is finally for.

Could it be that our anxiety and aggression, our desire to exert total control and exact maximum profit, follows from a basic inability to trust in God's beneficence and care? A case could readily be made that at the heart of our cultural malfunction lies a fundamental distrust in the goodness of God, a basic impatience with the ways of God and creation. Our temptation has been to step outside of our creaturely roles and try to be little gods ourselves, gods who will take by force the many things we should otherwise gratefully receive as divine gifts. This path, as our histories so clearly show, is the pathway of destruction and pain.

Sabbath reflection and observance can be a primary source of cultural renewal because it serves as the antidote to our misperception and destructiveness. Sabbath practices correct and refine our vision so we can see once again—as God saw at the conclusion of each day's creative work—how everything that is made is *very good*. Just as the Sabbath day is set apart and made holy, so can the thanksgiving and praise that are nurtured and promoted in Sabbath time and place become the basis for sanctifying the world and naming it holy.

My grandfather, I think, saw the sanctity in all things. He made time to see the goodness of God on daily display in his world. His vision was informed by his faith in God as One who is faithful to us and ever generous in the divine showering of gifts. This was no abstract faith. It was grounded in my grandfather's attention to and care of the earth and its animals. Though his life was not without hardships and pains, it was permeated by the kindnesses and the sacrifices of countless others—family, friends, neighbors, dogs, chickens, sunlight, rain, earthworms, and countless microorganisms he never saw. In the face of all this generosity and blessing, he would have asked: How can we not be grateful? How could we ever stop praising God when there is so much for which to offer praise?

If we, practically speaking, are to move into more grateful and worshipful ways of being, we are clearly going to need to slow down our living and become more attentive to the evidences of grace that surround us. We need to extricate ourselves from social and economic patterns that multiply stress and increase creation's suffering and destruction. A good starting point will be to form a new relationship with our food. We need to stop thinking of it as fuel, as a possession we control to further our own agendas. We will then need to become better informed about where our food comes from and under what conditions it is produced. Clearly, not all purchased food is bad or harmful. But if we want to be more responsible and sacramental in our eating, we need to form closer attachments to the food system.

The best way to do this, of course, would be to grow some of our own food. In this activity we learn concretely and palpably (through our stomachs!) the meaning of patience and faith, as we directly engage the ways of divine grace. Failing such gardening, we can make a deliberate effort to form relationships with those who do raise our food by frequenting farmers' markets or participating in community-supported agriculture (CSA) ventures. Here we can learn about, and hopefully directly see, the grace and the costliness of life.

As our sensitivities expand and as our appreciation for the complex, gracious ways of God grows, we will gradually find that gratitude and praise are irrepressible. To experience God's *hesed* or covenantal love in the midst of our practical living is to enter God's domain of blessing and joy. It is to see how our anxious, often wayward, striving represents an affront to the multiple levels of grace that sustain and nurture us daily. As we learn to attend and respond to the creative, vivifying action of God among us, we will learn to participate in a Sabbath singing that is now attuned to and extends God's rhythms of delight and peace.

2

The Meaning of the Sabbath

■ From a scriptural point of view, Sabbath observance is a matter of life and death. Having again gathered the Israelites at Mt. Sinai, Moses put Sabbath observance at the top of the list of things God has commanded them to do: "Six days work shall be done, but on the seventh day you shall have a holy Sabbath of solemn rest for the LORD; whoever does any work on it shall be put to death" (Exod. 35:2). This command reiterates a similar one given in Exodus 31:12–17, where we are told that Sabbath observance reflects a covenant between the nation and God, a covenant testifying to God's creative and refreshing power. Anyone who violates this covenant is cut off from the people and should die. Indeed, Sabbath observance is one of the key practices that will set Israel apart from all other nations. Insofar as Israel fails in its Sabbath responsibilities, it is entirely legitimate to claim, as Leviticus 26:34–35 does, that the pain, shame, and suffering of Babylonian exile are linked to the Israelites' "theft" of the land—their refusal to provide Sabbath rest for the land. By forfeiting the Sabbath, Israel ceases to be a nation devoted to and representative of God.

Given the utmost gravity of this command, it is clear that there must be more to it than simply taking a break from our regular routines. Sabbath observance is not merely a leisurely add-on to balance out an otherwise busy or frantic week, but rather the key that opens life to its fullest and best potential. We need to understand the overall religious trajectory that calls forth this command as something vital in the life of a follower of God and also dear to the heart of God. What does Sabbath observance aim to get us to see, feel, appreciate, and do? Why does the failure of Sabbath observance lead to religious breakdown and, we are to assume, the breakdown of life itself?

Sabbath Creation

When most people think about the Sabbath, they turn to the Ten Commandments, for here, in the fourth commandment, we are given explicit instruction.

> Remember the sabbath day, and keep it holy. Six days you shall labor and do all your work. But the seventh day is a sabbath to the LORD your God; you shall not do any work—you, your son or your daughter, your male or female slave, your livestock, or the alien resident in your towns. For in six days the LORD made heaven and earth, the sea, and all that is in them, but rested the seventh day; therefore the LORD blessed the sabbath day and consecrated it.
>
> (Exod. 20:8–11)

This command takes us back to the founding of the created order itself, showing us that Sabbath observance is not an incidental part of life. In fact it takes us to reality's core meaning and purpose, showing us what the whole of creation is ultimately for. By understanding the Sabbath we better appreciate who God is and what the character of all created life is. We begin to learn, in other words, what it is that God finally wants and expects of us.

To appreciate this, we need to change significantly the way we normally think about creation and God's creative work. As the story is usually told, God creates the whole world in six days by majestically speaking it into existence. God utters into ordered being light and darkness, the sky, waters and dry land, vegetation, sunshine and moonlight, and every kind of living creature in the sea, in the air, and on the land. On the sixth day, after creating the wild animals of the land, God creates *adam* (male and female humanity) according to God's own image. Humanity is then given the command to "be fruitful and multiply, and fill the earth and subdue it; and have dominion over the fish of the sea and over the birds of the air and over every living thing that moves upon the earth" (Gen. 1:28).

A logical progression in this six-day pattern suggests humanity as the climax, even the fulfillment, of God's creative work. After all, humans are created last in the line of succession, and God has saved the best—the most important—for last. With the creation of humanity God is finished, suggesting that we are the crowning touch. Humans, on this view, are the kings and queens of the heap because God has put us in charge. Everything below—the lakes, forests, soil, grasslands, fish, wild and domestic animals—has been given to us to do with as we see fit. We are to have dominion over every living thing.

This popular telling of the story is somewhat misleading because it overlooks important details and makes mistaken assumptions. For starters, it is tempting, especially in an industrial and technological age like our own, to assume our dominion means something like outright or total control. The Hebrew context, however, was agricultural. As the second creation story of Genesis 2:4–24 makes abundantly clear (by building upon the first), to be an authentic *adam* is to be intimately tied to the ways of soil (*adamah*), to be attuned to the soil's limits and possibilities. Farmers do not exercise dominion over their animals and fields by simply imposing or forcing their desires upon them. Dominion, if it is to be successful, depends on the farmer's cooperating and working with the life forms under his or her care. Indeed, dominion without patient and informed affection quickly leads to ruination, as fields are compromised and livestock become sick and die.

Far from being an excuse to do with creation as we want, the exercise of dominion is the practical training ground in which we learn to live patiently and attentively with others so that the mutual flourishing of all becomes possible. In a very important and practical sense, the vocation of humanity to have dominion will have to be worked out in the twin contexts of careful gardening, of tilling and keeping (even serving) the garden of paradise (Gen. 2:15), and the spiritual and moral work of conforming our lives to the life of God and thereby becoming the concrete manifestation or image of God (Gen. 1:26). As Terence Fretheim has proposed, humanity's most fundamental task is to share (however imperfectly) in God's continuing creative work of fashioning a livable and lovable world: "having dominion and subduing are understood *originally* as completely positive for the life of other creatures."[1] Indeed, as bound up in a common membership of creation, we are responsible in certain respects for the continuing becoming of creation.

Another crucial point is that God frequently stops to proclaim each day's creative work as "good." After the creation of everything together, its goodness is given special emphasis by God's declaring that "indeed, it was very good" (1:31). Clearly what is being communicated here is God's excitement and enthusiasm for what is being created. It thus makes sense to suggest, as Richard Lowery has, that God finds the whole of creation to be not only good but *delightful*, the occasion for intense and sustained joy.[2] It needs to be stressed, too, that God does not single out humanity as more delightful than all the rest. To be sure, humans will have a unique role to play in the ordering of creation, a vocation we can summarily describe as concretely representing and manifesting (imaging) God's intentions for creation. But their role does not by itself or automatically make them more delightful. In fact, and as the biblical witness makes abundantly clear, insofar as humans do not properly live out their vocation to be God's image on earth—when they destroy or become violent and arrogant—they become the occasion for God's greatest sorrow and pain.

Another detail, frequently unnoticed, is that God was not quite finished with the creation on the sixth day. Near the end of the story we are told that God finished once on the sixth day, but then again on the seventh. Why would there be a need to finish something twice? What would be the significance of a second finishing? Quoting from a midrash, the medieval rabbi Rashi claimed that after the six days of divine work creation was not yet complete. What it lacked, and thus what remained to be created, was *menuha*, the rest, tranquillity, serenity, and peace of God. In the biblically informed mind, *menuha* suggests the sort of happiness and harmony that come from things being as they ought to be; we hear in *menuha* resonances with the deep word *shalom*. It is this capacity for happiness and delight, rather than humanity, which sits as the crowning achievement of God's creative work. It is as though by creating *menuha* on the seventh day God gathered up all previous delight and gave it to creation as its indelible stamp. *Menuha*, not humanity, completes creation. God's rest or *shabbat*, especially when understood within a *menuha* context, is not simply a cessation from activity but rather the lifting up and celebration of everything.[3] Here we see God in a most personal (and exuberant) image, like a parent frolicking with a child and in this joy and play demonstrating an abiding commitment to protect, sustain, encourage, and love into health and maturity the potential latent within the child.

The creation of *menuha* is not a divine afterthought. Nor should it be viewed in a passive way, as a mere withdrawal from exertion. God's rest on the seventh day did not amount to a pulling back but rather a deep sympathy, harmony, and celebration with all that was there. In so delighting in the splendor of creation, God invites creatures to bask in the glory of the divine life. In a most important way, therefore, the creation of *menuha* gave to the whole of creation its ultimate purpose and meaning. Without *menuha* creation, though beautiful, would be without an all-encompassing, eternal objective, which is to participate in the life of God forever. And so what Sabbath *menuha* does is give us a positive vision of the world's goodness, a vision in which there is no fear, distrust, or strife. There is rather a celebration of, and a sharing in, God's own experience of delight.

Sabbath, being the climax of creation, is thus the goal toward which all our living should move. It is not merely an interlude within life, but rather its animating heart, suffusing every moment with the potential for joy and peace. It is the interpretive key that helps us understand what all the moments and members of life mean. It gives aim and direction to life so that we know how and where we are to move. Life's fullness or happiness cannot be achieved in the absence of divine delight. It is what God wants for us and for all creation. Abraham Joshua Heschel put this point beautifully when he said, "All our life should be a pilgrimage to the seventh day; the thought and appreciation of what this day may bring to us should be ever present in our minds. For the Sabbath is the counterpoint of living; the melody sustained throughout all agitations and vicissitudes which menace our conscience; our awareness of God's presence in the world."[4] Insofar as we genuinely experience Sabbath *menuha*, we catch a glimpse of eternity, a taste of heaven.

We can now begin to see why Sabbath observance is of the greatest significance and why our refusal to heed it is a great threat. In its practice, what we are finally doing is opening ourselves up to the happiness of God and letting God's intentions for *menuha* take precedence over our own ways. To refuse the Sabbath is to close the world in upon ourselves, by making it yield to our (often self-serving) desires and designs, and to cut ourselves off from God's presence and purpose. In our arrogant fantasies of dominating the whole creation, we forestall life and precipitate death. To forget or deny Sabbath is thus to withhold our lives from their most authentic purposes in God. It is to claim that our worrisome ways are better or count more than the intentions of God. It is to put ourselves at the center of creation—the very definition of sinfulness—rather than God's own delight.

Sabbath Freedom

One way to read ancient Israelite history, but also Christian attempts at church formation, is as a long, complex narrative in the ways of faith and faithlessness. Our propensity to sin—to put ourselves and our agendas, fears, anxieties, and desires first—is so strong and pervasive that in many cases we do not even appreciate that by denying God we also deny life. We do not see, let alone acknowledge, how our sin wreaks havoc with the biological and social world and brings pain to others and to God. We need help: prophetic witness, ritual remembrance, and concrete practice that will cause us to see, then critique and reorient, our action and desire in light of God's overall plan. For this purpose the Sabbath is vital.

Consider the way Deuteronomy's version of the Ten Commandments casts Sabbath observance. After beginning much like the version in Exodus 20, with the command that all people and animals rest from their work on the seventh day, this version ends: "Remember that you were a slave in the land of Egypt, and the LORD your God brought you out from there with a mighty hand and an outstretched arm; therefore the LORD your God commanded you to keep the sabbath day" (Deut. 5:15). This ending, rather than tying Sabbath observance to the fulfillment of creation's overall goal and purpose, links the Sabbath to the founding and the purpose of Israel as a nation liberated by and called to serve God. Israel should not be like Egypt, and one of the clearest ways to see the difference will be that Israel practices Sabbath and Egypt does not.

As is well known, the liberation of Israel from Egypt was a formative event for the nation. By vanquishing Egyptian power and might God would now make possible an alternate form of power, one founded on peace and fidelity rather than violence and distrust. In order for this power to become manifest in Israel's economic and political life, however, the people would first need to learn what it means and what it entails. The training period began with forty years of wandering in the wilderness.

> Remember the long way that the LORD your God has led you these forty years in the wilderness, in order to humble you, testing you to know what was in your heart, whether or not you would keep his commandments. He humbled you by letting you hunger, then by feeding you with manna, with which neither you nor your ancestors were acquainted, in order to make you understand that one does not live by bread alone, but by every word that comes from the mouth of the LORD.
>
> (Deut. 8:2–3)

The reference to manna is especially important. While in the wilderness the Israelites had to learn what it means to depend upon God for every good and perfect gift. They had to understand that the blessings they lived by did not come from the work of their own hands but were instead concrete signs of God's care and concern.

One of the clearest ways to consider this is again to think about food. Food is not a "product" but a gift that we must nurture. Ultimately, as every good farmer and gardener knows, whether or not we will have food is beyond our control. The best that we can do is practice patience and trust, attention and responsibility, before the processes of life and growth. In the wilderness the Israelites would start their religious formation by learning that with something as basic as food they could not live from the might of their own hands. They were entirely dependent upon God to provide for them. And this God did every day. Each morning, as the Israelites awakened, they would find a day's supply of manna on the ground for them to gather. It was always enough to take care of their daily needs.

The Israelites were expressly forbidden to hoard more than a day's supply (perhaps with the intention of profiteering from the excess or from the fear that God would not in the end prove trustworthy). If they did, they would discover that the excess had spoiled by the next day.

The central point in all of this is that for our livelihood we must learn to depend on God, recognizing that without God the basic processes of life—respiration, digestion, decomposition, growth, and health—would come to an end. Our power, in other words, is never really our own. It is a borrowed power—a gift—since it depends upon, moves within, and always partakes of God's power. Manna is but one example among the many gifts we need to be sustained every day, gifts like clean air, photosynthesis, soil regeneration, energy, communal support. When we forget these gifts, or when we fail to see them *as gifts* and mistake them to be ours by right or by our own effort, we falsify who we are. We overlook the fact that our lives are everywhere maintained by a bewildering abundance of kindness and sacrifice.

So that we would not forget, God set aside the seventh day as an occasion to rest, remember, refocus, and give thanks. On the sixth day of each week God sent down a double portion of manna, manna that would not spoil the next day, so that the Israelite nation as a whole could gather to worship on the seventh. Worship is the natural, near inevitable, outgrowth of a life that no longer esteems itself to thrive through "the might of my own hand" (Deut. 8:17) but instead through the grace of God. When we worship, we give our full attention to God, acknowledging that if left to ourselves alone our world would crumble and fall. God is worthy of our praise and thanksgiving because God is unfathomably generous and kind, having created a world worthy of our unending joy and delight.

Clearly, this does not mean that we will fully comprehend God's kindness and its distribution or understand why it is sometimes laced with unspeakable pain and suffering. Nonetheless, Sabbath worship is the time and space when we most fully appreciate and declare the goodness of God. It is the time of thanksgiving and praise, when we humbly confess our dependence on God's generative but also sometimes terrifying grace. It is the occasion when we acknowledge and exalt the sustaining presence of God everywhere already in our midst. Those like the dullards in Psalm 92, who fail to worship, are thus massively blind and ignorant about the many ways in which God provides and conserves. Forsaking all appropriate humility, they arrogantly and destructively assume themselves to be the captains of their own fate and that of the world. They have no appreciation for the costliness and the splendor of life.

Sabbath Rest and Peace

The Israelites knew as well as anyone that people can declare God's goodness with their lips but then with their hands and feet manifest the preeminence of self. For this reason their Sabbath teaching included well-developed social and economic directives, beginning with the clear command that all work stop on the seventh day. It is easy, especially in our work-obsessed culture, to underestimate the significance of this injunction. But if we remember that the Israelite economy was predominantly agricultural, then this command takes on special significance.

When I look back at the farming community in which I was raised, I am astounded by the fact that family members and neighbors stopped work on Sundays. At most times of the year this was not a big deal, but during harvest seasons it most certainly was. In a farming economy the produce of the land, and thus the lion's share of the farmer's sustenance and income, comes in at specific times of the year. The window in which harvest can occur is limited, due to changing ripening and drying conditions. Every day during harvest is thus precious and not to be squandered, for whatever is not appropriately harvested spoils and registers as lost income, as lost livelihood for the family and sustenance for livestock. If the farmer gave up work to rest and bad weather set in and spoiled the remaining harvest, the costs were truly high.

One would think that Sabbath rest would thus be the occasion for considerable anxiety, especially in an agricultural economy. But in our community worry and fret did not overcome the Sabbath aim of rest and refreshment. To be sure, the farmers might worry about whether they had made the right choice by not going into the fields on Sunday, but such worry would reflect a distrust in God's ability to provide and take care of them. Worry and anxiety would be byproducts of a fundamental doubt of the goodness of God, a suspicion that maybe God's grace is limited or not enough. My experience of farmers at that time, however, is that they experienced daily multiple examples of God's goodness and power, most basically in the germination and growth of crops and the birth and health of livestock. To be sure, crop failure and disease, as well as painful death, were perennial possibilities, but the experience of farming overwhelmingly taught the beneficence of grace. (It is no accident that as farming has turned into agribusiness, the practice of Sabbath rest for farmers, animals, and the land has come to an end.) If the farmer is honest, and thus appropriately humble, he or she will recognize that there is much more to be grateful for than there is to fear. Authentic rest becomes possible, even in the midst of harvest time, because it is informed by the palpable, concrete understanding that God provides. The means of divine care, whether in plant and animal cycles of birth, growth, decay, and death or in the kindnesses of kin and community, are ample and clear for those who care to notice.

Rest is not simply about stopping. When we stop from our work, what we are really doing is exhibiting a fundamental trust and faith in the goodness and praiseworthiness of God. Of course faith is not a guarantee of special divine favor. But we cannot delight in God's provision for us if we are at the same time worried about whether or not God cares for us. Sabbath rest is thus a call to Sabbath trust, a call to visibly demonstrate in our daily living that we know ourselves to be upheld and maintained by the grace of God rather than the strength and craftiness of our own hands. To enjoy a Sabbath day, we must give up our desire for total control. We must learn to live by the generosity of manna falling all around us. The patterns of our current economy, no less than the Egyptian models of success, make such trust very difficult. Deep down, we all have difficulty with the idea that we live through the mercy of divine gift. We prefer to think that we live through the might and control of our own exertion.

Sabbath observance thus gives us the time and the space to take a considered look at what our work is finally about. Our temptation is to think that we live through our own effort and that the goods we enjoy are ours because we have earned and deserve them. A moment's reflection can quickly dispel that illusion, as everywhere we look we can see the generosity of others: earthworms aerating and rebuilding soil, plants turning sunlight into energy, family providing for us since birth, teachers looking out for our children. The list of kindnesses goes on and on, but we often fail to notice. We are simply too busy with our own agendas and our sense of self-importance.

The Sabbath asks us to notice. It compels us to reconsider and question with depth and seriousness what all our striving is ultimately for. Will it be the work representative of a slave economy, an economy that knows no Sabbath rest or delight but only unremitting toil and inescapable violence? It is time for us to realize that good work is work that invites the presence of God and that enables us all together to experience God's own *menuha*. It is, as Ellen Davis wisely suggests, "done in the remembrance of God's work of creation, and also in imitation of it."[5] Does our exertion bring honor to God, or is it at cross-purposes with the life-giving, life-celebrating ways of God? This is the sort of reflection and reorientation that Sabbath observance asks us to undertake.

Sabbath Justice

Sabbath teaching proclaims rest for the *entire* household. Again, the full significance of this command is easily lost on us, because we no longer experience the household as a body that includes extended family, workers (even slaves), and farm animals. By proclaiming that everyone should rest together, we begin to see some of the revolutionary potential latent within a Sabbath sensibility. Put simply, *the rest of one person should not be at the expense of another's exhaustion or toil.* Having just come from the experience of slavery in Egypt, where the wealth and success of a minority clearly depended on the systematic abuse and oppression of the majority, the Israelites would have readily seen that Sabbath teaching is about the liberation of all to share in the goodness of God. God's grace is not reserved for the select, powerful few. It extends to the whole community of life, even to strangers, animals, and the land itself.

It is difficult for us to imagine an economy and society without oppression and violence. Everywhere we look we see that some get ahead because others fall behind; this becomes especially apparent when we acknowledge that human wealth is frequently at the expense or exploitation of natural and worker capital. That we do not often see the connections between upward and downward mobility does not mean they do not exist. The question, therefore, is whether we can make progress in the ways of a nonexploitative economy. How do we need to think and act so that all creation can share in God's *shabbat* or experience God's *menuha*?

We begin to see some practical implications when we attend to scriptural references to the Sabbath year. The basic issue always is whether God is believed to be sovereign, perceived to be in control and able to provide. Consider the command from Exodus 23:10–11:

> For six years you shall sow your land and gather its yield; but the seventh year you shall let it rest and lie fallow, so that the poor of your people may eat; and what they leave the wild animals may eat. You shall do the same with your vineyard, and with your olive orchard.

In a condition of fear and distrust, we are tempted to amass as much power and possession for ourselves as possible, believing the more control we have over our own fate and those of others the more secure we will be. This is the path of violence, the way that leads to the oppression and abuse of others. It is also a way that reflects fundamental ingratitude. The acquisition of wealth by some inevitably leads to the impoverishment of others, and it is precisely this impoverishment that God cannot abide. Oppression and need are a direct affront to the goodness and mercy of God. God's sovereignty demands the extension of God's care to everyone and everything. It requires that creation have the freedom to be itself, to be what God has wanted it to be since the dawn of creation. If we believe that God is sovereign, we have to assume that God will provide for everyone and that any effort to hoard for ourselves is a denial of this divine provision.

We can see now that Sabbath teaching carries a strong emancipatory thrust. It begins most practically when the Israelites are told that Hebrew slaves must be freed from their slavery without debt in the seventh year

(Exod. 21:2). They are to have the opportunity to reestablish themselves as free and equal partners in the community of creation. So too with the nonhuman creation of domestic animals and the land and vegetation itself: they must have freedom to come out from under our unremitting demands, as when animals are left to rest and refresh themselves or fields are left to lie fallow. As we cease from our steady toil, we learn the valuable lesson that the whole of creation does not exist exclusively for us and to meet our desires. Creation belongs to God. It is at its best when it fulfills God's intentions for it. We are at our best—we most exhibit the image of God—when our work aids those intentions and when it supports and maintains the generosity of God. So Lowery is exactly right when he says, "The law of release, *shemittah*, then is the exact opposite of being tightfisted toward needy neighbors. It is a concrete gesture of opening the hand to the poor."[6]

The egalitarian and emancipatory thrust of Sabbath teaching became most pronounced in the vision of Jubilee, the "Sabbath of Sabbaths," for it is here that people were to return to their families and to their ancestral lands. As suggested by Leviticus 25, it was possible for individuals and families to fall into hard economic times and thus lose their lands or be reduced to slavery. In an agricultural economy, particularly when it is a subsistence economy, mounting debt is a hole few are able to crawl out of on their own. Without land or the freedom to work it, the poor essentially become destitute, while those who have power and money grow their wealth and landholdings at the poor people's expense. This growing discrepancy between rich and poor, and the exploitation that often enables it, are a direct affront to the generosity and care of God, which is why the prophetic literature and the Psalms frequently rail against those who continually seek to amass greater and greater fortunes. What the vision of Jubilee asks (whether it was satisfactorally answered in historical reality is hard to know), when it demands that land lost to poverty and misfortune be returned, is that the vision of God's care for the poor become an economic reality and not simply a theological platitude.

The psalmist writes:

> Happy are those whose help is the God of Jacob,
>   whose hope is in the LORD their God,
> who made heaven and earth,
>   the sea, and all that is in them;
> who keeps faith forever;
>   who executes justice for the oppressed;
>   who gives food to the hungry.
> The LORD sets the prisoners free;
>   the LORD opens the eyes of the blind.
> The LORD lifts up those who are bowed down;
>   the LORD loves the righteous.

> The LORD watches over the strangers;
>> he upholds the orphan and the widow,
>> but the way of the wicked he brings to ruin.
>
> (Ps. 146:5–9)

The psalmist's happiness here described must be understood as practically connected to the Sabbath recommendations offered in Leviticus 25. Happiness, liberty, justice, and Sabbath rest all come and go together.

> And you shall hallow the fiftieth year and you shall proclaim liberty throughout the land to all its inhabitants. It shall be a jubilee for you: you shall return, every one of you, to your property and every one of you to your family. . . . You shall not sow, or reap the aftergrowth, or harvest the unpruned vines. . . . You shall eat only what the field itself produces.
>
> (Lev. 25:10–12)

Sabbath and Jubilee teaching thus combine the profound theological truth that the world is best when it lives for God and God's pleasure, and a concrete, practical vision that calls each of us to arrange our economic patterns and priorities so that they enable all members of creation to participate in the *menuha* of God. The Sabbath is not a break from life but rather a profound theological lens that enables us to get a better look at all of it. In its observance we commit ourselves to honor the presence of God in all things and to participate in the ways of life and health.

Keeping the Sabbath really is a matter of life and death. When we forsake the Sabbath, what we are finally doing is closing ourselves off from God's life-giving and life-sustaining grace (see Ps. 104:27–30), demonstrating that we think we can live by ourselves and from our own might. Though we no longer physically kill those who violate Sabbath observance, we have to acknowledge that this path, because it is fraught with anxiety, fear, and worry, will inevitably lead to violence as we attempt to expand and make total the reach of our control and power. The security and comfort we think we are achieving will finally be hollow, because they come without the delight that follows from experiencing the world as God experienced it at the dawn of creation, and as God still yearns to find it today.

3

From Sabbath to Sunday

■ It is tempting for Christians to think that with the birth of Jesus Christ Sabbath observance became something of the past. After all, at various points in the Gospels we see that Jesus ignored Sabbath law so that he might do his work. For instance, Jesus defends his disciples when they pluck grain on the Sabbath (Matt. 12:1–8), while he himself on the Sabbath heals a man with a withered hand (Matt. 12:9–14) and a crippled woman (Luke 13:10–17). Moreover, Jesus notes that "the sabbath was made for humankind, and not humankind for the sabbath; so the Son of Man is lord even of the sabbath" (Mark 2:27–28, cf. Matt. 12:8 and Luke 6:5). This seems to suggest that the Sabbath is put beneath him, is perhaps even put away for good. Though Sabbath observance may have been of value and importance to the Jews, the time inaugurated by Christ no longer requires it.

This interpretation of Jesus's life and ministry, and its relation to the Sabbath, is a serious mistake. To be sure, historical evidence shows that the development of the Christian Sunday was not simply a gospel way of observing the Fourth Commandment. But this does not warrant the view that Sunday served as a better or improved replacement for the Sabbath. From a theological point of view, we should insist on continuity between the Jewish Sabbath and the Christian "feast day." Jürgen Moltmann rightly argues, "The Christian Sunday neither abolishes Israel's sabbath, nor supplants it. . . . The Christian feast-day must rather be seen as the messianic extension of Israel's sabbath."[1] Put succinctly, in the person of Jesus the Sabbath aspirations that heretofore guided the Israelites now find a most visible and compelling expression. If we want to see, feel, hear, taste, and touch what God's delight in creation concretely amounts to, we can do no better than to consider the life and ministry of Jesus Christ. As the early medieval pope Saint Gregory the Great put it: "For us, the true Sabbath is the person of our Redeemer, our Lord Jesus Christ."[2]

Creation in Christ

Uniquely Christian Sabbath teaching takes us to the inner heart of the world's meaning, for in the incarnation of God in Christ the whole of creation is given a renewed, redemptive focus. Just as the Sabbath represents the climax or fulfillment of creation, so too Jesus reveals what God's intentions for life have been all along. What does it mean to be a creature of God, and what are we to do with the life given us? How do we best live the life that will bring delight to God and health and peace to the whole of creation? The life and ministry of Jesus enable us to answer these questions in new ways, for now all of reality is to be reinterpreted in terms of the cross and the community of forgiveness and healing it makes possible. If we remember that, according to a Christian point of view, it is through Christ that "all things came into being" (John 1:3) and that "through him God was pleased to reconcile to himself all things, whether on earth or in heaven, by making peace through the blood of his cross" (Col. 1:20), then it becomes clear that creaturely life is most authentic or at its best when it shares in Christ's own life, when it moves in a trajectory that lines up with his. As Christians we are to take our cues from Jesus on what is good and valuable for us to do, because he gives us a fresh glimpse and a practical manifestation of what the *menuha* of God looks like.

Pope John Paul II's apostolic letter *Dies Domini (The Day of the Lord)* makes very much the same point: Jesus does not obliterate Sabbath teaching but reframes it so that we can see once again, with renewed emphasis, what creation's ultimate meaning is. John Paul writes: "The Paschal Mystery of Christ is the full revelation of the mystery of the world's origin, the climax of the history of salvation and the anticipation of the eschatological fulfillment of the world." The Lord's Day is the key to every day that has been, that is now, and that is yet to come. Christ is the inner meaning of all history. He gives it its most authentic direction and purpose. Every day of our lives should be lived through the life of Christ, since it is in terms of his loving and sacrificial life that we now know what life is for. Christ calls us and the Holy Spirit empowers us to live lives that are abundant and free, no longer given over to arrogance, anxiety, ill-health, or violent struggle. Jesus comes to us not as a thief who wants to kill, steal, and destroy; rather, he says, "I came that they may have life, and have it abundantly" (John 10:10).

"Creation in Christ" inaugurates a fundamentally different ordering of reality from the one we might choose for ourselves. Our ways of ordering, premised as they are on self-promotion and the tools of exploitation and control, inevitably lead to violence and death. The way of Christ, which is the way creation is supposed to be, inaugurates a new kind of reality no longer dependent or parasitic upon violence. James Alison has put this well: "It is not as though creation were a different act, something which happened alongside the salvation worked by Jesus, but rather that the salvation which Jesus was working was, at the same time, the fulfillment of creation."[3] Jesus's resurrection life puts in place a new kind of life that has implications for everyone. Clearly, the abundant and full life that Jesus represents is not yet completely realized in our midst. Here and now we will continue to experience pain and suffering. But in the midst of this pain the cross stands as a sign of both judgment and hope.

To appreciate this point we need to understand how the cross "shows up our world for what it really is, what we have made it. It is a world in which it is dangerous, even fatal, to be human; a world structured by violence and fear." Jesus most fully reveals what it is to be human: to lose ourselves in love and to be obedient to what love calls us to do. But it is precisely our fear of loss of control and our lack of faith that compel us to crucify him and thus keep at bay the obedience to and gratitude for God's love that his life represents. The stunning claim of Christianity, however, is that our violent efforts do not defeat God's love for us. Christ's resurrection means that love keeps coming and is made available to us so that the relations frayed or destroyed by us can again be made healthy and whole. "Through the risen Christ the Spirit is poured out upon all men, or, to put it another way, the relationship between Jesus and the Father . . . is extended to all men."[4]

Sabbath Salvation

If we are to speak this way we must broaden the scope of Christ's redemptive work beyond personal postmortem salvation to include the restoration of creation as a whole. Here we do well to remember that early Christians thought of the Lord's Day as a "little Easter" celebration. Sunday is a feast day because in it we celebrate the "new creation" made possible by the resurrection of Christ from the dead (scripture suggests that Christ's resurrection took place the first day after the Sabbath, making Sunday the first day of the week). Christ's ministry is not an add-on to

God's creative work. Rather, and given the gospel's proclamation that all things are created through Christ, it represents the fulfillment of created life. Through the power of the resurrection all things can become "new," meaning they can become most fully what they were always and originally meant to be. We become sick and tired, distorted and destroyed, as we turn away from God's original creative intention. Christ's hand in creation, now combined with Christ's earthly ministry, lets us know how we can be renewed and thus show forth what God wanted of us all along. By following Christ's example we gradually enter into the *menuha* of God.

If this interpretation is correct, we need to move beyond the highly individualistic notion of salvation that many of us assume—that Jesus is significant because of the salvation he makes possible for individual believers. It is important to understand that the church early on worked to combat precisely this tendency. The work of Christ extends to and links up with the whole of creation. Maximus the Confessor (580–662), for instance, argued that God's incarnation in creation was present from the beginning of time as the divine *logos* or truth permeating an intelligible, ordered world (the *logoi* of creation). In Jesus Christ this same *logos* "became flesh" and thus joined the ranks of humanity. Far from being an abrupt interruption in the orders of creation, the life of Jesus Christ is thus in seamless continuity with it.

This view casts salvation within a much larger framework. The *logos* of God is not at work solely within human lives; it is present and effective throughout all creation. In the person Jesus we see God's interaction with creation expressed in a most intimate, intense, and bodily way. As John McDade summarizes it, God's nearness to creation presents salvation "as the restoration of creaturely equilibrium, and subordinates human reality within the framework of the world's natural processes." Christ, in other words, does not take us out of creation to save us, but rather saves us precisely by enabling us to enter more fully and more harmoniously into it, and then to find in this deep immersion the reality of God. "The specific history of God's action in Jesus is, therefore, the focus of intensification, the moment within the process which illuminates the whole, and which exemplifies the nature of the Creator/creation relationship."[5]

With this encompassing context in mind, it becomes all the more significant for us to recall that Jesus performed many of his miracles on the Sabbath. The question is why. Was it simply to irritate the religious leaders of the day? A better explanation is to see the miracles as specific people—creation in miniature—being set right to be what God intends. In the miracles of healing, feeding, restoration, exorcism, and raising from the dead, Jesus is revealing creation's inner directionality or purpose and bringing it to completion. Jesus is communicating God's continuing creativity in the world, a creativity informed by divine love and care.

John's Gospel has Jesus say, on the Sabbath no less, "My Father is still working, and I also am working" (5:17). Jesus, in other words, is filling a lack or repairing a distortion in creation. His whole life and his going to death represent the putting right of creation. His pronouncement from the cross, "It is finished," is a reference not simply to his own life but to the life of the whole world. Again, Alison has stated this well: "Creation itself has been brought to fulfillment by his self-giving up to death in order to open up for us a creative way by which we may come to participate fully in creation. It can be understood, then, why the resurrection happens on the first day of the week, in the garden. Creation has started again, a creation in which the tomb is empty."[6] What is finished is not simply a personal life but the whole complex network of patterns of behavior that lead to violent crucifixion. What is opened up is the possibility of resurrection life, life that is completely open to the peaceful, reconciling ways of God.

The depth and breadth of God's salvific intentions become clear if we consider the story of Christ's healing of the ten lepers recorded in Luke 17:11–19.[7] While walking between the regions of Samaria and Galilee, Jesus is approached by lepers who call out for mercy. They need care and help not only because they are physically ill but they also bear the pain of social alienation. As physically unclean, they are cut off from membership in the wider social community. In their bodies and in their relationships, they are disfigured and denied, unable to live out the goodness of God's creative intention. Sensing their desperate need, Jesus instructs them to show themselves to the priests, knowing that their reentry into the larger social body will depend on the priests' judgment and proclamation of their physical cleansing.

Luke tells us that as the lepers went to the priests they were "made clean." The term used is *katharidzō*, which means to purify but also to declare ritually acceptable. What we see here is that Jesus was concerned with these persons' physical, bodily health—the leper who comes back to thank Jesus sees that his body is "healed" or "cured," restored to its proper biological functioning (*iaomai*)—but also with their restoration as full members into the social body. We do not live alone or as rugged individualists. We need each other and depend upon the sympathy and support we provide to each other. In a very real sense, the health of human living, its success and fulfillment, depends upon the health and wholeness of the many relations that bodily existence requires.

The broad and deep conditions of health implied here need to be emphasized. Luke's story tells us that health is in membership rather than isolation. Membership with whom? It is tempting to limit the range of our memberships to as small a circle as possible, because this is a natural way to maximize control over our own lives. This is why we prefer to be part of groups that are like-minded or make few demands of us. The ministry of Christ, however, shows us that our memberships go far and wide to include those who are not like us—people of other cultures and races (the leper who thanked Jesus was a Samaritan), the unclean, the poor, the sick, the disenfranchised—those who do not count according to our scales of importance. It even extends to nonhuman life, for we are embodied and cannot possibly live well if the nutrients that feed us—animals, plants, water, soil, and air—are sickly or in decline. We need to remember the principle that was well-known in ancient or traditional cultures: bodily health includes the health of the many bodies, human and nonhuman, we necessarily live with. We are members of creation, and our well-being depends on the health of the whole creation. We are foolish if we think that we can be whole at the expense or in violation of the broader creation. Wholeness is a precondition for health, which is a precondition for delight and celebration. There can be no complete *menuha* in a context of dismemberment or devastation.

There is, however, a third, and most expansive and fundamental, dimension to the healing that takes place in Luke's story. Jesus engages the Samaritan leper who returned to give thanks by asking what happened to the other nine. He wonders why they have not thought to stop to offer similar thanks and praise. Jesus is clearly dismayed by their blindness and their unwillingness to acknowledge and act upon the fact that our health, indeed the means of all our living, is finally a gift. We need to ask if our own ingratitude would not be a cause of God's continuing dismay. Though these lepers experience a dramatic bodily healing (the social healing has not yet taken place) as their leprosy is cured, the fact of the matter is that every time we eat, drink, and breathe, we experience and participate in the grace of health. Every time we experience the help of the social body, we encounter the blessings of social membership. All wholeness, in the end, is a reflection of a gracious God who cares for us all by showering us with the gifts of bodies, food, and community. To be healthy in any way whatsoever is, whether we appreciate it or not, to bear witness to God's continuing involvement in the maintenance and wholeness of creation. If we are attentive, our whole lives should be one long act of thanksgiving and praise.

Luke ends this story with Jesus's telling the leper, "Get up and go on your way; your faith has made you well." This time the leper's health is termed *sōdzō*, which is the word used for salvation. The leper's life is "saved" because it is now made well and preserved in terms of God's own life. In an important sense, the leper's faith has marked his own living with a participation in God's life. His trust in the provision of God, his thankfulness for God's care, and his loud praising (Luke 17:15) of God's graciousness indicate that he no longer sees his life in terms of himself.

He is no longer like the dullards of Psalm 92: he has shifted his frame of reference from himself to God's overarching intentions. His gratitude and praise to God confirm that a Sabbath sensibility is dawning within his mind. The wholeness of bodily and social relations made possible by Christ's healing word is now made complete by a wholeness of relationship with God. In Luke's view there is no such thing as partial wholeness. The abundant life that Jesus proclaims entails the conviviality and peace of the whole creation before its Creator.

Put succinctly, salvation, understood as the goal toward which all life moves, is integrally tied to *menuha* as the experience of God's delight in creation wonderfully made. Salvation is the always new recapitulation of the tranquillity, peace, and joy that marked the first Sabbath. To be saved is to participate in and enjoy God's life as it is intended for all creation. It is to realize here and now as much as possible what God has wanted and hoped for us from the beginning of time.

New Life

Another way to understand Christ's work as the origination, continuation, and fulfillment of God's creative design is to recall that for the early church father John of Damascus, the work of creation could best be understood as God's "making room" for what is not God to share in God's joyous and peaceful life. God's creative work, on this view, resembles one long and lavish act of hospitality, a welcoming and a sustaining of life within a context of unfathomable grace and goodness. In an important sense, Christ's ministry is the radical, most fundamental and concrete, expression of what divine, but also earthly, hospitality must be for us: the welcome of all to the banquet of life; service to all in need and who suffer; and the celebration of our life together blessed by God's continuing care. Jesus models for us in a most practical way what God's original and abiding hospitality looks like. Our most important task as disciples is to open the table of welcome to others, not because the table of gifts is ours to give but because we are always already beneficiaries of and witnesses to grace upon grace. When we do this, we say yes to God's invitation to joy.

Our gathering together on Sunday is thus of the deepest significance, for in it we are empowered by God to extend the love that sustains and brought creation into being. When we offer this gift of love to others, we are really creating a space for them to become themselves and to most fully realize their God-given potential. In this work we mirror God's own creativity, which simply and without coercion lets the world be. "Love is the space in which to expand, and it is always a gift. In this sense we receive ourselves at the hands of others. . . . To give love is to give the precious gift of nothing, space. To give love is to let be."[8]

Sunday is the Lord's Day, which means that on this day we set aside time to make sure that Christ is indeed the Lord of our living and not we ourselves. We gather together so that we can better learn what Christ's lordship means for us in the midst of our everyday living. We begin to see that the life of Christ was above all devoted to the overcoming of forces that destroy or disfigure life—hunger, disease, demon possession, anger, envy, alienation—and the promotion of personal and communal dispositions and practices that nurture and facilitate a complete or maximal life. As the apostle Paul puts it, those who follow Christ will manifest the fruit of the Spirit: love, joy, peace, patience, kindness, generosity, faithfulness, gentleness, and self-control (Gal. 5:22–23). These are the traits of those who have made Christ's ministries of feeding, healing, exorcism, reconciliation, sharing, and inclusion part of their own daily walk.

Sunday is the day when Christ's followers most visibly gather to pledge their allegiance to the ways of Jesus. Yet the activity of being a church, the work of discipleship and hospitality, is not confined to that one day. Pope John Paul II suggests that we view Sunday as the training ground that prepares us to go into the week and there mirror Christ: "the whole of Sunday becomes a great school of charity, justice and peace." The real test of our allegiance and commitment occurs in the everyday, as we work with colleagues, raise our kids, care for our elderly, construct our built environments, tend to our lands and waters, and do our shopping. These are the places where the feast of the "new creation" is either realized or not. These are the times when Christ's resurrection power comes to fruition or not.

Our world mostly fails to mirror the health of wholeness that would constitute God's salvation. Though God's resurrection power has been unleashed in the person of Jesus Christ, we still await the time when God's "new creation" is fully realized. As Romans 8 puts it, creation is in a state of "eager longing," waiting to come out of its current condition of suffering and futility. It is in "bondage to decay" (v. 21), due to the effects of sin and violence that have been at work since the time of Adam. For this reason several of the early church fathers, Basil and Augustine among them, referred to Sunday as the "eighth day." Though Sunday is the first day of the week, in terms of the seven-day creation of the world it also stands beyond creation as its final summation or conclusion. We should, therefore, think of Sunday as an intensification of the Sabbath, a new beginning for creation, because it represents "the age to come." It is an eschatological reality, which means that on this day Jesus has opened up new possibilities for genuine life, possibilities that have been set in motion but are not yet fully complete. The *menuha* of God that shone upon God's original creation will once again, because of the redemption made possible by Christ, usher in a time and place of peace and delight. Augustine, writing very near the end of his *Confessions* (and referring to 2 Thess. 3:16), called this "the peace of quietness, the peace of the sabbath, a peace with no evening" (13.50).

This way of speaking reinforces the Sabbath view that the goal of all life is to find its rest in God. What distinguishes Sunday from the Sabbath is that the path to this rest is through the cross of Christ. The incarnation of God in Christ opens up fresh possibilities for realizing a Sabbath vision here and now. Hebrews 4 suggests that as Christians we are called to enter into the rest made possible by Christ. Christ is for us the image of eternity, the true light of the world that enables us to see clearly and without ambiguity what creation means and what it is finally for.

Given that Christ's resurrection rest follows after the suffering of the cross and is a vindication of the power of life over death, the Eucharist, the weekly celebration of the risen Christ, is central to Sunday observance. As we eat the body broken for us and drink the blood shed on our behalf, we proclaim the living power of God to break the bonds of sin and death that pervert and destroy creation's memberships. When we celebrate the Eucharist, we express our hope in the power of God's love to enter and strengthen our relationships with each other so that they better reflect God's peace and delight. Here we acknowledge and live out God's intentions for us and thus bear witness to God's primordial joy in a creation that is "very good."

It is helpful to link the celebration at the "Lord's Table" with the divine hospitality that marked, and continues to impress itself upon, God's first creative work. The experience of the Eucharist is an experience of communion. It is the time when we recall and celebrate our many memberships with each other and with God our Creator. We prepare with acts of forgiveness in which we acknowledge and commit ourselves to end the anxiety and arrogance, the pettiness and aggression that testify to our perennial sinfulness. At the Lord's Table we open ourselves to the gifts of God and each other, recognizing that it is through these gifts, and not through our own efforts or by our own right, that we truly live. Rowan Williams says it well: "In the resurrection community, the fellowship of the Spirit, the creative and sustaining power of God is shown to be identical with the compassion and forgiveness that renews and reconstitutes the relations of human beings with each other."[9]

The forgiveness here talked about is of a most practical sort. I recall once hearing a woman describe how at her church, before the moment of Communion, the entire fellowship formed a large circle. Each member then went down the line to every other member, asking if there was need for forgiveness between them, and if so offering it. Clearly this was a lengthy affair, as encounters between some people revealed conflict, animosity, or jealousy. But it was a valuable moment in the life of the congregation, making clear and honest the relationships that bind us to each other, and allowed healing and strengthening to take place. When we wound each other, whether knowingly or not, we disfigure and maim the whole body, making it less likely that it will be a community of hospitality for others.

Sunday peace and rest, much like Sabbath peace and rest, extend to the whole creation. The Leviticus code made it clear that animals and the land needed their rest too: true rest is never at the cost of another's exploitation or misery. Given that we are embodied beings, our living is always implicated in the living of other, nonhuman bodies. We need to pause and look carefully and patiently—going down the line of habitats and animal life—to determine how our actions impair creation's memberships.

Paul clarifies that resurrection hope is not restricted to the human community. All creation will be set free from its bondage to decay. "We know that the whole creation has been groaning in labor pains until now; and not only the creation, but we ourselves, who have the first fruits of the Spirit, groan inwardly while we wait for adoption, the redemption [apolutrōsis—setting free or deliverance] of our bodies" (Rom. 8:22–23). What Paul is suggesting here is that sin prevents the members of creation from becoming what God has intended for them to be. As a result, the membership of creation as a whole is thwarted. Its existence, rather than causing God delight and joy, ushers in pain and sadness. The hope of the resurrection—the hope that love's power is victorious over the ways of sin—lets us know that creation as a whole and we ourselves are not fated to live this way forever. The ways of forgiveness and sacrificial love make possible our liberation from the distortion and destruction that sin is, so that we can again live in ways that will cause God to delight. This redemption is not for disembodied souls that escape or rise above creation. Rather, Christ's redemptive power is always at work at the level of our bodies, and the bodies of all members of creation that together make life possible.

Sunday, far from being the obliteration of Sabbath teaching, represents a profound rearticulation of God's overarching purpose and plan for creation. Sunday is our day of joy, for here we remember our memberships one with another and commit ourselves to the health and wholeness—the salvation—of physical and social bodies, of communities and creation, made possible by Christ's resurrection power and redeeming love.

4

The Practice of Delight

■ The fact that Sabbath observance has a low priority for many people in our society indicates a profound confusion about what the Sabbath means. It ought to be our highest priority and our deepest desire, because *the experience of delight is what the Sabbath is all about.* What could be finer or more desirable than to share in God's own *menuha* or to participate in healthy, convivial relationships that mark the reconciling, redeeming presence of Christ among us? That Sabbath observance is often accompanied by dour faces and lengthy lists of prohibitions, or that Sabbath days are often laden with the stresses of the workaday week, suggests that in our planning and practices we have made some serious errors in judgment.

A number of forces at work in our culture aim to prevent us from experiencing true delight (more on this in the next chapter). The church has, sadly, largely capitulated to these forces and in so doing has deprived itself of practices that lead to our collective health and joy. Sabbath observance ought to and can be one of the church's primary ways of witnessing to God's emancipatory and peaceful ways in the midst of a violent culture that knows no rest. Too often what we see instead are churches held captive by insecurity and given over to anxiety and the denial of life.

To realize Sabbath's potential, we need to focus for a moment on delight's inner meaning and manners. In what ways does the practice of delight result in relationships that are godly and conducive to *shalom* and joy? How can the experience of delight become the animating heart of a Sabbath sensibility that infuses every aspect of our practical living?

The connection between delight and the Sabbath should not be hard to draw, for in expressing delight we show our joy and great pleasure in the gifts of God. To take delight is finally to relish the goodness and beauty of God's work and to see in each other the trace of God. It is to recognize and appreciate that we are all gifts to each other and that our mutual welcome forms the basis for convivial life together. This is why the exercise of delight readily slides into acts of praise and thanksgiving. How can we not be thankful or express praise once we are aware of the countless kindnesses that feed and inform our living?

Delight is not merely a passive phenomenon. It presupposes the internal personal preparation whereby we put a halt to the controlling, self-serving impulses that would reduce others to our personal satisfaction or fancy. If we want to show true delight, we must first tame our self-ambition by learning the arts of detachment and genuine attention. Only then will others appear to us as genuinely other, as creatures with an integrity of their own that commands respect. Only then will they come to us in the freshness of God's grace rather than the sameness and predictability of our own (often narrow) expectations. Delight is always delight in another. If it is to be genuine, it must work actively to affirm and make room for others to become what God intends for them to be. As we see others for what they really are, concrete expressions of God's unfailing love, they can become occasions for our care and celebration.

God's Delight

The model or pattern for our practices of delight, of course, is God, who, throughout the divine creative work but also at its end, took immense pleasure in what was made. Let me emphasize that God took pleasure in creation itself, in its freedom and integrity, and not simply in himself or in creation understood as an extension of himself. Terence Fretheim underlines creation's integrity when he says, "Israel's God is intimately and pervasively present in the created order but in such a way that God allows the creation to be what it was created to be without strict divine control."[1] God beheld the world, all that was within it but also its great potential, and proclaimed it "very good"! The scriptural account of creation testifies to a divine exuberance that builds and flows into the works of creation. If we remember God's creative work as being the concrete manifestation of divine love, then it is impossible to think that the creativity itself, but also its visible effects, would be anything but delightful and a joy to behold.

We find it difficult to imagine that God delights in creation because we have gotten used to the deistic idea that God is distant from earth and for the most part uninvolved, that God is not near, not on close, familiar terms with us, because creation runs entirely according to its own laws and in terms of its own energy. But as the biblical witness makes abundantly clear, there is an intensity of intimacy between God and creation that overwhelms our attempts to keep God at bay. God wants to be with the creation, wants to see it succeed and experience joy and peace, and so again and again God enters into covenant relationship with it and with us despite our faithlessness. Clearly, scripture paints God as One who is affected by being in relation with creatures and who desires that all creation be well.

Nowhere is the sense of God's fierce fidelity more striking than in the book of Hosea, where, despite Israel's disloyalty and shame—imaged as whoredom—God promises to love and care for his people:

> I will make for you a covenant on that day with the wild animals, the birds of the air, and the creeping things of the ground; and I will abolish the bow, the sword, and war from the land; and I will make you lie down in safety. And I will take you for my wife forever; I will take you for my wife in righteousness and in justice, in steadfast love, and in mercy. I will take you for my wife in faithfulness; and you shall know the LORD.
>
> (Hos. 2:18–20)

God's loyalty and love are founded on creation's fundamental goodness; notice that this covenant extends beyond humanity to include the whole of life. As the concrete manifestation of God's own love, all created life is forever and fundamentally delightful and good—at least in God's eyes—despite our worst efforts to mar and disfigure it.

The sense of creation's loveliness also comes through powerfully in Proverbs 8, where the Wisdom of God, personified as feminine, created before and present at the foundation of the world, speaks of the freshness and beauty of all that was made.

> When he established the heavens, I was there,
>   when he drew a circle on the face of the deep,
> when he made firm the skies above,
>   when he established the fountains of the deep,
>   when he assigned to the sea its limit,
>   so that the waters might not transgress his command,
> when he marked out the foundations of the earth,
>   then I was beside him, like a master worker;
> and I was daily his delight,
>   rejoicing before him always,

> rejoicing in his inhabited world
> and delighting in the human race.

(Prov. 8:27–31)

Imagine the enthusiasm and excitement that are being communicated back and forth between God and Wisdom as God brings yet one more aspect of the divine goodness into being. They are like beaming parents unable to contain their delight when contemplating the potential of new life, and then seeing their children thriving and doing well. In the face of such wonder and splendor, the automatic response is pure joy. Proverbs advises us to heed God's Wisdom, so that we too might share in this fundamental experience of delight.

In our better moments, when we put aside our insecurities and our continual grasping for personal advantage, we all can recognize the freedom and pure joy that comes from such delight. Think about those moments when a child or friend, despite many personal, physical, or social obstacles, achieves a difficult goal. This is cause for celebration, for the person's God-given potential has been realized and made manifest for others to share. What makes such celebration even sweeter is to know that we have aided in the person's triumph. To celebrate fully with another entails that we have been involved enough in this person's life to see the cracks and openings through which God's grace and love shine through. We can share with them in their joy because, as Paul says in 1 Corinthians 12:14-26, we have also shared with them in their pain and distress.

If we find occasions for genuine celebration to be infrequent, it may well reflect our uninvolvement in others' lives. Years ago, with the help of my wife's corrective vision, I noticed myself growing quickly impatient with my young children. I found their antics annoying and frustrating, even a source of personal embarrassment. Actually I had let my work and my sense of self-importance take control of me, with the result that I spent less and less time with my kids. I did not really know where they were coming from, what their routines or struggles or needs or sources of happiness were. Lacking this connection, I could not see when they accomplished or experienced something wonderful, nor where I might help them. I hampered their joy by not helping facilitate it. I also hampered my own because I was in no position to see the good that was happening in their worlds.

God's delight, but also our own, has clearly been hampered by the effects of sin. Scripture speaks repeatedly of how our faithlessness contributes to the neglect and destruction of human relations and of creation and thus to the diminishment of creation's splendor and beauty. Nonetheless, God's faithfulness endures. God promises to renew creation:

For I am about to create new heavens
    and a new earth;
the former things shall not be remembered
    or come to mind.
But be glad and rejoice forever
    in what I am creating;
for I am about to create Jerusalem as a joy,
    and its people as a delight.
I will rejoice in Jerusalem,
    and delight in my people;
no more shall the sound of weeping be heard in it,
    or the cry of distress.

(Isa. 65:17–19)

The blessing that creation itself is, as well as God's continuing generosity in showering gift upon gift, is the permanent sign that God cares for us and finds us worthy of abiding love.

Beneath God's blessing and faithfulness, God finds the whole creation lovable and a delight. When we promote relationships that strengthen and deepen our memberships with one another—as when we commit ourselves to regularly helping a person who is disabled, or when we periodically offer to clean up (and thus make more lovely) a patch of natural habitat disfigured or marred by us—God is honored and glorified.

In some sense we need to learn to feel God's sorrow in our blindness and perversity in mishandling or abusing the relationships that make our lives meaningful and rich. When we scorn God's blessing by greedily taking more when we already have enough, or by abusing gifts for our own glory rather than God's, or by destroying the relationships that bind us to each other and to God, we bring sadness to God and ruin to ourselves. For our waywardness is the proud and stupid refusal to acknowledge that we live by the grace of God's blessing rather than through our own might. Whereas God's power brings about the thriving (though not always completely understood) goodness of creation, our own power, which often takes the form of a rebellious antipower, leads too much to creation's diminishment. Insofar as we set ourselves up to be little gods of our own, we invariably pervert and distort God's power of life into a power of death.

If we are to be happy and complete, we must return to God and see ourselves and the whole creation through divine eyes. The divine perspective on creation is that it is delightful, good, and much more than sufficient to take care of our every need. As we move into God's presence by learning to live in ways that mirror God's own life-affirming and life-building ways—by lifting up those who are ill, hungry, poor, lonely, or alienated through acts of healing, feeding, generosity, visitation, friendship, and reconciliation—we will again recover the joy that marked creation's seventh sunrise.

> You show me the path of life.
>> In your presence there is fullness of joy;
>> in your right hand are pleasures forevermore.
>
> (Ps. 16:11)

The historical appearance of Jesus Christ continues this theme of delight. The life, ministry, death, and resurrection of Jesus are "good news" because Jesus is the strongest affirmation of the fundamental goodness and loveliness of all God's creative work. This is why John the Baptist, while still in his mother's womb, "leaped for joy" (Luke 1:44) at Mary's greeting and announcement that she would give birth to the Son of God. It is why the angel appeared to the shepherds saying, "I am bringing you good news of great joy for all the people" (Luke 2:10). In Jesus, God's joy is made concrete. Through his ministry we see the practical manifestation of God's love for us and thus catch a glimpse of why God made anything at all.

When Christians practice the love of Christ, they enter into God's own life. They begin to see others in the way God sees them, as worthy of care and in need of mercy and hope. *Christlike ministry forms the practical context in terms of which the world can appear as lovable and delightful.* John's Gospel makes the connection clear when Jesus says, "If you keep my commandments, you will abide in my love, just as I have kept my Father's commandments and abide in his love. I have said these things to you so that my joy may be in you, and that your joy may be complete" (John 15:10–11). Our distance from God, a distance defined by our sinful, self-promoting ways, makes it impossible for us to see and engage others the way God would. The effects of our sinful engagement are permeated by jealousy, fear, anxiety, aggression, sadness, anger, and pain. When we enter into the life of God by following Christ's commandments, however, we can learn to handle others the way God would want: with charity, kindness, sympathy, mercy, attention, forbearance, and forgiveness. The net effect of this transformation in our vision and action is that we will experience creation the way God does, as concrete expressions of divine love, and thus with joy. This divine joy is what finally makes us complete. As followers of Christ we should "rejoice with an indescribable and glorious joy" (1 Pet. 1:8).

Our Delight

Let us now step back from this brief scriptural account of the place of delight in the life of God to see how delight might become manifest in our own practice and life. As we have seen, delight goes hand in hand with joy and love. Recall that God's delight in creation followed from God's loving work of bringing creation into existence. Love became concrete in the divine creative work, which means that this same love was reflected back to God in works of creation that are good and beautiful. Seeing this goodness and beauty brought joy and delight to God. Had the original creation been flawed, sick, or a failure—perhaps a manifestation of cosmic violence or struggle rather than unfailing love—God's response would not have been delight. The goodness and beauty of creation, that which makes it a delight to us, stems from the fact that it is the concrete manifestation of God's love and hospitality. Few have understood this as well as the seventeenth-century poet Thomas Traherne: "Lov is the true Means by which the World is Enjoyed. Our Lov to others, and Others Lov to us. We ought therfore above all Things to get acquainted with the Nature of Lov—for Lov is the Root and Foundation of Nature: Lov is the Soul of Life, and Crown of Rewards. If we cannot be satisfied in the Nature of Lov we can never be satisfied at all."[2]

Because delight is grounded in the love of God, our capacity for delight is not to be identified with our ability to experience personal pleasure. This distinction is crucial, as we often find pleasure in sinful ways or are tempted to make personal pleasure the gauge to mark the value of things. For instance, it may give me pleasure to see someone I know, perhaps a fellow contestant for recognition or a particular honor, falter or come to shame. But this would be an evil form of pleasure, born out of wickedness or a desire to do harm rather than show love. Though we might say that we *delight* in another's downfall, we are really falsifying the term. Delight follows upon and is a reflection of the goodness of another. True delight would be expressed in another's success rather than failure, for it is God's desire that all be well.

Saying that delight is not to be identified with pleasure does not mean that delight is without pleasure. Clearly what God delights in is also pleasing to God. The reason we don't begin from the perspective of pleasure, however, is that its focus is too much on ourselves. Pleasure quite often starts and ends with how an experience makes us feel. Its point of reference is often too narrow, not enough focused on the integrity and wild beauty of others. The goodness of creation does not narrowly depend on the possibility that it is good for me (this was one of the important lessons learned by Job) but more broadly on the affirmation that a good, loving God made it. This point is crucial, for in many instances, particularly occasions of pain and suffering, we are not in the best position to evaluate the goodness of what lies before us. God's goodness, how and why it appears the way that it does, is in the end a deep mystery to which we must submit with appropriate humility. Our problem is that we do not always or enough engage others for God's sake or glory, and thus our pleasure is susceptible to becoming false or even sinful. The principle of all our delight, that which makes it genuine and authentic, is that it must be grounded in and keyed to God's own delight in setting creation into motion. Whenever we experience *genuine* delight, God will necessarily be honored and glorified as a result.

The meaning and goodness of others, that which makes them delightful, emerges in our loving interaction with them. We can't really take delight from a distance or in a condition of apathy or ignorance. Here we need to recall God's steadfast love for creation, a love that will not let us go despite our faithlessness and self-imposed pain. God loves us because God *knows* us at our deepest, most fundamental level as the self-expression of divine love. We don't really know others until we understand them in this light. David Bentley Hart has said that the practice of delight forms the indispensable context for genuine knowledge or understanding of others: "It is delight that constitutes creation, and so only delight can comprehend it, see it aright, understand its grammar. Only in loving creation's beauty—only in seeing that creation truly is beautiful—does one apprehend what creation is."[3]

If we are to see others with this depth, we must be prepared to get close to them and learn to see them for what they are, rather than for what we want them to be or in terms of how "useful" or pleasing they are to us. The humility, patience, and commitment required for this are increasingly difficult to practice in our culture of haste and mobility. A superficial estimation of others stops short at the first sign of behaviors or character traits that annoy us, frighten us, or hurt us. We are called to move beyond the superficial. Just as God looks beneath our ugly and annoying sinfulness and sees a creature reflective of and continually in need of divine sustaining love, so we too must learn to see every member of creation as a gift of God, a reflection of God's love. For this we must find practical, regular occasions that will help us overcome superficiality in relationships.

Here the example of Jesus is again instructive and helpful. Jesus was well known for his association with society's outcasts. Unlike us, he did not seek out relationships that would position him to move up an economic or social ladder. His commitment to the sick and hungry, the deranged and ostracized, shows that his first priority was to be with others as they were, to try to understand them in their terms, and then to facilitate *their* joy by alleviating their suffering and pain. Jesus's compassion for others was founded on a disposition of perpetual welcoming, making others the guests of honor. For good reason, therefore, Jesus calls those who would be his followers to "deny themselves and take up their cross daily and follow me. For those who want to save their life will lose it, and those who lose their life for my sake will save it" (Luke 9:23–24). Jesus is saying that we let our egos get in the way of having caring, compassionate relationships with others. Too often we place our own perceived good above the needs of another, with the near inevitable result that others are harmed to suit our ends. Jesus's point is that if we were to seek the good of others, the whole of creation, and thus we ourselves, would be well. Thus in Luke 12:22–31 Jesus tells us not to worry so much about ourselves. As we seek God's kingdom, where all is finally governed by joy and peace, all the things we need will be given to us. What grounds and sustains our hope is the promise of God's love and faithfulness.

Delight Is in the Details

We are too much social climbers, angling and jockeying for position within an ever-changing hierarchy of prestige. We continually compare ourselves with others, seeing who is more successful or popular or beautiful. This is a losing position to be in, since there will always be somebody who compares better in some area. It is also theologically naive, because it assumes that God sees us in a similar hierarchical manner. When we recognize that we are all sinners, there is no cause for boasting and no need for competitive comparisons. In God's household all members are equally important.

It will help us to figure out the many ways in which other people and creation itself are vital to our own flourishing. This will require a detailed knowledge and accounting of how the presence of others intersects with and enables our own living. Ask yourself, *Do I really have a clear grasp of what people do for me, go through for me, and contribute to me?* Such an accounting will require that we make time to get to understand people more deeply.

For me this happened several years ago, when I was working in a homeless shelter in Chicago's near west side. Though we had been in operation for several weeks, as a staff we hardly comprised a well-working machine. I don't think any of us relished being there. Then one day our supervisor wisely called a meeting of all staff. Our job was simply to talk to each other, find out about our backgrounds, and articulate why we were there and what we aimed to accomplish in our work.

To many outsiders, I am sure that our supervisor's decision to halt work for a chat session would have appeared wasteful and extravagant. Yet this encounter with each other had a profound effect. Even the homeless men and women who came to the shelter responded by asking, "What happened?" We began to work together better, and we found that we enjoyed being with each other as we carried out our tasks. Laughter was heard more regularly, and a willingness to help each other became apparent. Getting to know each other, even if it was not the deepest knowledge, made a tremendous difference in our work environment.

Consider, as another example, our treatment of people who are not thought to be of much use to society. The writings of Jean Vanier and Henri Nouwen note that we easily dismiss mentally disabled individuals because they are not productive economic citizens or scientific and intellectual pioneers. Because of their "deficiencies" it is easy for us to dismiss them as beyond our concern or incapable of inspiring delight. For those who work closely and affectionately with the handicapped, however, nothing can be further from the truth. Naturally there are moments of frustration, but those who get to know such folks with a measure of depth and commitment will see the love of God at work in them. In fact, their spontaneity, and the fact that they bring fewer agendas to their engagement with others, means that they more readily see and enjoy the gifts of God around us. They can be our teachers in the ways of delight.

Josef Pieper has said, "Joy is the response of a lover receiving what he loves."[4] This succinct aphorism expresses well the relationship between our experience of delight and the depth of our love. Joy is the fruit of loving action that draws us ever deeper into the world. As we experience creation with greater depth and in finer detail, we encounter a world sustained by God's love and care. Perhaps the joylessness so evident in our culture reflects the superficiality of our relationships with others. The call to delight is a call to embrace the whole world, even its unpleasant parts and moments, and find there the love of God at work. Equipped with this understanding of God's creative presence, we are put in a position where the fullest affirmation of reality is possible.

Delight follows from an affirmation of another's God-given goodness. The qualifier *God-given* is important lest we think that affirmation is narrowly limited to what pleases or suits us. When viewing from a more divine perspective, we will discover that we can be open to welcome, even cherish, a wider range of reality than what is merely useful or pleasurable to us. Even events like sickness and death, or seemingly useless pain, that are occasions for sadness or grief can be affirmed if they are received in light of the goodness of God. The most fundamental and important question here is, do we trust that the ways of God are shaped through and through by love? Without this affirmation we cannot pronounce the "amen" that signifies our willingness for things to be as God wishes.

When we note the connection between our ability to say "amen" and a genuine affirmation of the world, how little this word passes our lips should give us pause. That we do not say "amen" very often or in diverse contexts indicates that we are not truly happy with this world or this life.

We perpetually yearn for a different life, a "better" one that more closely meets our expectations and desires. But why should another world or another life, even one of our own choosing, be more pleasing? Does not every life have its troubles and cares? This yearning is a betrayal of the Sabbath and a denial of delight. Rather than giving rise to praise and thanksgiving, much of our yearning confirms a deep-seated ingratitude. It also reveals our unwillingness to love others the way God loves them, in ways that restore them to beauty and health.

It is important that we not understand delight as a passive phenomenon. We must continually position ourselves in such a way that the affirmation of others in their goodness becomes possible. Pieper extends his statement about delight and love with this: "For man cannot have the experience of receiving what is loved, unless the world and existence as a whole represent something good and therefore beloved to him."[5] To claim others as beloved entails that we have gotten sufficiently close to them so as to see the many dimensions of a grace-filled life. It is to see them as belonging to us and we to them.

Festive joy is impossible when we are naysayers, when we find fault with others or think them not good enough. "Festivity lives on affirmation."[6] Our capacity for delight depends upon how deeply we have entered into the divine life and taken it as the point of departure for our engagement with the world. The practice of delight presupposes a radical departure from all utilitarian calculation of benefits to self and a devotion to the building up and strengthening of others.

Saying "amen," we now see, takes us to the heart of Sabbath celebration, because there can be no true celebration, no true worship, without acknowledgment of and submission to the ways of God. If we enter into Sabbath time believing we know better than God and are best suited to take care of life on our own, then our worship is a sham. Any words of thanksgiving or praise we utter are false, for they fail to affirm life as a reflection of the love of God. When we offer praise and thanksgiving to God, we acknowledge that God's grace makes our living possible and is sufficient. Like the psalmist, we admit that in the end we owe all life to God:

> These all look to you
>> to give them their food in due season;
> when you give to them, they gather it up;
>> when you open your hand, they are filled with good things.
> When you hide your face, they are dismayed;
>> when you take away their breath, they die and return to their dust.
> When you send forth your spirit, they are created;
>> and you renew the face of the ground.

> (Ps. 104:27–30)

As a community of worship, we try to make sure that our praise and thanksgiving are not tainted by the assumption that we could live better if we were in charge. This assumption is arrogant and hugely destructive, as our histories of tyranny and oppression show us. Authentic celebration and worship take the focus off us so that God, as the giver of every good and perfect gift, can be praised. As we recognize that life comes from God and does not depend on our own frantic or stressful exertion, we can finally enter into that deep rest and contentment that constitutes life at its most complete and authentic pitch.

In the words of Michael Hanby, "Only a joyous people can sustain pointless activity, festivity, and rest. Only a people who can sustain pointless activity, festivity, and rest can be joyous."[7] Delight makes rest possible, for in its practice we have given up the need to secure the world and our existence by our own hands or in terms of our limited (often arrogant) rational accounting. Our culture would lead us to believe that joy is something we create and earn through our own effort. The teaching of the Sabbath offers us a strikingly different path, a way that begins and ends with the love of God as the foundation for any and all goodness in life. Joy and delight are not something we bring about. They follow from our grateful acceptance and affirmation of God's gracious care. To practice delight we do not, indeed must not, rely on ourselves alone. Instead we learn the art of opening ourselves up and making ourselves available to the creative love that permeates and sustains us all. We all learn to look differently, with the eyes of God. The practice of delight is the life we perform under the inspiration and full acknowledgment of God's gracious presence in the world, a presence that lets us know we are loved and that invites us to extend this same love to others.

5

The Decline of Delight

■ Today's entertainment industry is the clearest indicator that we are growing incapable of experiencing genuine delight. This sounds counterintuitive, because while we are in the throes of our entertainment we generally think we are having a good time. The attraction of many forms of entertainment, however, is that they give us release or an escape from life, whereas the experience of delight follows from a deeper immersion in and affirmation of it. Many people feel an intense need for hyperbolic and artificial stimulation, thrill, or distraction, while numerous forms of entertainment entail entrance into a virtual or "made-up" reality vastly different from our own. The implication is that we find the reality we are normally in unworthy, dull, or perhaps even despicable. Entertainment industries have become so lucrative and ubiquitous precisely because they are tapping into a widespread desperation people feel in daily life.

Given this cultural context, it is not surprising that the practice of delight has grown increasingly difficult. Rather than knowing the deep joy of relationships that are healthy, strong, and amply celebrated, and the happiness that follows from contributing to goals that are worthy and ennobling, we have settled for being amused.

Adventures in Artificiality

How did we come to such a pass? What are some of the cultural forces that keep us from experiencing the delight that would complete us and render our embrace of others a joy? In lieu of offering the long and very complex response that these questions deserve, this chapter will briefly highlight some of the features of contemporary life that mitigate, even militate against, the practice of delight.

A good place to begin is with the artificiality that imbues much of our social life. The patterns of our living have become highly stylized, mass manufactured, and scripted. What we choose to do and how we do it are increasingly determined by external forces like institutions, technology, the media, bureaucratic requirements, and economic necessities that have the effect of fragmenting or standardizing our memberships. Our activity, especially in an age of the spectacle or image, is highly circumscribed by the changing dictates of political, consumer, artistic, even religious fashion. Our living has become highly mediated, without spontaneity or directness. Moreover, the bonds that necessarily and beneficially connect us to each other have become weak and precarious, tenuous and provisional, because today's global marketplace requires people to be flexible, transient, rootless risk-takers who can seize whatever opportunity comes their way.

Observing post–World War II American society, Wendell Berry writes: "It is ephemeral, shallow, fashion ridden, diseased by the sense of its own transience. It is always feverishly changing its appearances and its affectations, and yet at its heart it has always the same fear, the same boredom asking to be diverted by such changes. It is stifling."[1] The artificiality Berry describes is composed of two main elements that at first do not seem to go together at all: change and boredom. One would think that boredom would be a feature of a stagnant or still world rather than a changing one. But that is not the case. The word *boredom* came into our language precisely at a time of rapid economic and cultural change: the Industrial Revolution. With industrialism, and now even more with globalization, the predictable and familiar patterns of Old World communities were left behind so that various forms of economic and social opportunity could be pursued. To be "modern" is to seek out the new and not feel constrained by the old.

Berry's account focuses on the mass migration of farmers to the city that was well under way for decades before World War II and accelerated rapidly after it. Farmers and their children were lured by the anonymity, excitement, and "opportunity" (a word virtually synonymous with "escape") that cities seemed to offer. Most of all, the city came to be identified with the potential for success, defined almost entirely in monetary terms. Whereas farms were places of hard, predictable work, cities were places where innovation, the product of risk and daring, could provide us with unheard-of goods. In a certain respect, cities represented the "unknown": they were quite unlike rural communities in that their inhabitants were mostly unknown, and thus not responsibly tied, to each other. Berry describes this period as a "migration in the direction of money." Society "was conceived as a pyramid on which the only desirable or honorable or happy position is the top. People not at the top envied those above them, despised those below them, and apologized for themselves."[2]

Once reality is defined in terms of this quest for success—the big house, fancy car(s), large retirement fund, vacation getaways—several spiritual effects necessarily follow. Foremost among these is "the pragmatization of feeling." What Berry means by this is that personal and social life are driven by the increasingly individualized pursuit to "get ahead" and "make something of ourselves." Because getting ahead requires all our energy and time, humanizing emotions—those feelings that most define us as social, embodied creatures made in the image of God, "pleasure in small profitless things, joy, wonder, ecstasy"—must simply be sacrificed. Equally significant are the pervasive forgetting and casual disparagement of the relationships that make our living possible: communal memory and support, friendships, healthy soil, clean water and air, kinship with nonhuman life, and the handing down of traditional skills and wisdom. What matters most is what will increase our earning potential. But our goal, the top of the social and economic pyramid, has a very hypothetical and elusive nature; there can be no limit, no point where we reach "enough," because the top is defined in ever-changing, relative terms. And the journey takes a heavy personal toll: unremitting work, postponement of intermediary pleasures, neglect of family and friendships, stress-induced illness, and loss of a sense of home.

One would think that with this flurry of frantic activity there would be no time for boredom. But this is because we misunderstand the true nature of it. Boredom is not the same as having too much time on our hands. Its root goes much deeper, to what Hanby identifies as a failure to find the world and each other compelling or interesting.[3] We find the world boring because we don't see very clearly why it is valuable and good or how and why we practically and beneficially belong to it. We are bored with ourselves because we don't think that what we do really matters much or is of life-giving interest to others. And so we become disengaged from each other, wandering about in a fog of diminished hopes and expectations. Not knowing what to do, and having become suspicious of what our society encourages us to do, we sit around, hoping to find some inspiration. What we have here are the ideal conditions for the entertainment industry to pump us up with artificial stimulation, excitement, and false hope. Finding our personal world intolerably dull, we crave, create, or live vicariously through spectacles of intrigue or destruction (real or imagined) that will help us feel alive. Boredom has rendered us vulnerable, easy prey to market-driven or politically manufactured desires and promises.

We can now begin to see why *boredom* should enter our vocabulary and spiritual makeup precisely at the point of our increased potential for economic success. A phrase from Michel de Montaigne can serve as our most succinct clue: "He who has his mind on taking, no longer has it on what he has taken."[4] The more we obsess about personal success, especially defined as the accumulation of wealth, the more our focus is narrowed to the possession and consumption of goods rather than the goods themselves. What we have ceases to be *good* in the strong sense of the term, because what matters most is not the thing itself but our possession of it. Things "count" or have value primarily and insofar as they can appear in a positive ledger column. They cease to register for us as gifts of God's gracious love, the very quality that renders them a source of delight.

If we remember that delight is made possible by our loving and deep affirmation and embrace of others, that it follows from and bears witness to the God-given goodness in another, then it is easier to see how our desire to possess or be entertained by others works against our joy in them. We cannot take delight in others, whether friends or family, pets or plants, watersheds or wastelands, because we no longer have our minds on them. We do not, for the most part, behold them as creatures of God, manifestations of divine love, generosity, and help.

In our utilitarian society, things matter when they function to promote personal or social (most always economic) benefits. And our purpose as consumers is to keep the stock market on the rise. But is not utilitarian benefit one of the flimsiest hooks on which to hang each other's worth? Once I recognize that my perceived value rests on how I can bump up another's bottom line, it is easy to feel that whatever less tangible worth I have is a sham. Anxiety and hopelessness, boredom and despair are the inevitable result. The whole membership of creation is now compromised, because it ceases to find its value in the grace of God.

Being Less

One useful way to chart our culture's movement away from the authentic practice of delight is to show how human life can be characterized in terms of *being, having,* and *appearing.* These three terms represent different ways we have for identifying ourselves and our place in the world in relation to others. They presuppose different priorities and ways of acting in the world. Depending on the mode we are in, each will produce a differing conception of reality and thus a more or less direct and honest (and delightful) encounter with the grace of God.

In the mode of *being,* people live as closely to the sources of life as possible. They work actively to acknowledge and assume responsibility for

67

the many processes and memberships (social and biological) that make human living possible. To return to being, it is vitally important that we overcome the illusion that we live independently or autonomously. That illusion creeps in on many levels: in the rugged individualism of American culture, the fierce independence of seekers of fortune who forsake all to "make their own way," rites of passage (the college experience foremost among them) that aim to separate us from the priorities and patterns of family and tradition, or a preference for anonymity in the big city or big church. At the heart of our quest for autonomy lies a desire to be on our own, to live life on our own terms. What we often fail to realize is that autonomy is but a hair's breadth away from alienation. In wanting to live on our own, we find ourselves lonely and emotionally cut off from each other.

Of course, not all forms of independence are simply bad. What is damaging is the arrogant assumption that we could live best without the many layers of support and relationship that make every life possible. None of us can live well alone. We need the nurture and help that come from soil and water, microbial and animal life, flowers and vegetables, parents and siblings, extended family and friendships, teachers and leaders—all gifts from God. Who we are is a feature of how and to what degree these elements intersect with our own living. We live honestly and well when we acknowledge, respect, take care of, and dwell responsibly within these many memberships. Insofar as we live deeply within these many layers of relationship, we open ourselves to the experience of the love of God, for it is precisely through these memberships that God's care and concern are made practically and concretely manifest.

We do not appreciate well enough how changes in modern daily life make close, direct engagement with others much more difficult. I have already alluded to one such change: the historically unparalleled exodus of the vast majority of Western people from rural to urban or suburban life. Suburban and urban life thickly insulates us from the vast panorama of geophysical and biological life that is absolutely indispensable to human flourishing. As urbanites we have little direct, practical contact with energy or food production. We don't know where our food and fuel come from or how they are produced, since companies mediate or broker our access to them. Because the sources of heat, power, and nutrition are out of sight, they remain largely out of mind. It now becomes much more likely that they will be abused, for we are not informed or available to protest their abuse. Equally important, we may come to think that these elements of creation are not vital to who we are. Our experience of ourselves, of God, and of creation has been dramatically distorted. We simply fail to appreciate our immersion in a larger, meaningful flow of life.

Another important change has to do with the institutionalization and systematization of much modern life. The ways we experience each other and the world have become much more framed and scripted than ever before. Bureaucratized educational programs, with their heavy emphasis on routine and curriculum, take freshness and spontaneity out of the learning experience. Students do not pick or approach their subjects of study in ways that naturally follow from or flow back into patterns of daily and communal life. Our access to reality, whether in the domain of science, social relationships, religious faith, or even the weather, is filtered through systems of experts or professionals who set the terms for engagement and understanding. More and more we depend on others to tell us how we should perceive, feel, and think.

In this context it is important to note the role that technology has played in mediating our access to each other and to reality. Various technological devices work together like a ubiquitous filament that runs through our lives. Some developments, like the Internet and high-speed travel, make it possible for us to encounter domains of reality that would have been beyond the access of most common people in the past. Yet the character of these and other technological encounters is invariably more superficial and thin. Reality is compressed and its complexity reduced (and thus rendered more shallow) so that it can be manageably presented on a screen or through a disc or wire. A technological presentation is necessarily a framed or cropped reality. Someone else chooses how and what we will hear or see, which means that an encounter with the depth of reality—possible only through multiple engagements over time—is traded for the ease (and often anonymity) of the touchpad, keystroke, or glance. So while technology opens up certain kinds of experience, it renders that experience more dependent on a class of technicians and their bosses, who filter or promote it.

One of the great dangers of a technological age is that the ease and power it affords dramatically alter the way we conceive and engage reality. Think for a moment about power. To be the owner and operator of a technological device means we have considerable control over the world we engage. We can, with the ease of a switch, radically alter a landscape or turn off a relationship. Rather than develop our own skill sets through hours of training and discipline, we can simply purchase the machine's talents and thus employ them at will. Our technopower makes it unnecessary to take the time to engage deeply and learn from others. Why bother learning to perform a task when a program can do it for us? Why deal with an irritating colleague when we can simply log off? The mystery, integrity, and resistance of a foreign world of others is forcefully overcome or dissimulated so that the operator's agenda can proceed unabated. Moreover, the sense that we belong to each other, are interdependent, and need each other's help evaporates in the march to individual success.

A similar process of disengagement is at work in how we experience health, illness, and even death. Modern medicine, for all its benefits, has changed the way we experience our bodies and our bodily connections to a wider world. Social critic Ivan Illich points out that in traditional societies doctors played the role of helping patients interpret their pain and discomfort in terms that would foster internal and external harmony or balance.[5] Bodies were understood organically rather than mechanistically and thus necessarily drew their health from a wide array of others. Beginning in the seventeenth and eighteenth centuries, however, doctors began to focus much more on isolatable parts or organs that could be manipulated or treated. Regimens of treatment (now in hospitals) required the patient to be cut off from the social and biological contexts that normally rendered them whole. Pain was simply something to be killed or excised from human experience. The doctor's role was now much like that of the mechanic. Listening, encouragement, and personal support become harder and harder to come by in this increasingly lonely and clinical setting.

Though we will return to questions of pain and suffering in the next chapter, here it is important to appreciate how this clinical development gives us a conception of a body made up of many isolatable parts and subject to all manners of disease and attack. What we know of our bodies often has little to do with how we intuit or directly experience them. Indeed, for many people a trip to the doctor becomes a source of great confusion, as diseases and treatments are discussed in a language that is esoteric and unintelligible. Our bodies cease to be our own. They are the business of health care professionals, the property of hospitals, the foils of the pharmaceutical industries. Death, an experience that is universal and entirely normal, comes to be something we face alone. Rather than being a social event in which the depths of our relationships are clarified and celebrated, death is denied and the dead are hidden. The handling of death is assigned to morticians and funeral professionals.

My concern here is not to turn back the clock on medicine. It is, rather, to remind us that we find it increasingly difficult to think and feel ourselves as properly mortal, contingent, interdependent beings and to see in our mortality an occasion for the refinement of a more realistic estimation of ourselves and for training in the skills that best build and strengthen our relationships with others: attention, sympathy, mercy, forgiveness, kindness, honesty, fidelity, and hope. We don't develop these arts or skills ourselves because they have been taken over by specialists and professionals and then fed back to us in radically altered, institutional, prepackaged forms. The result is a growing distance between life as it is in the raw and life as it is mediated to us. What life is, how we feel it and define it, has been co-opted by experts, political pundits, technophiles, think tanks, gurus, and marketers.

The Mere Display of Life

The reduction of life into prepackaged forms flows directly into the mode of living characterized by *having*. Here we tend to talk about ourselves and our world not in terms of how we necessarily and practically relate to others but rather in terms of how we possess them. Possession is a key factor: in the *having* mode who we are is a feature of what we own. Again, the terms of our possession occur on multiple levels, beginning with our bodies. Bodies are things we have rather than what we are as a result of family inheritance and biological influence. They are open to a variety of techniques of manipulation and improvement that can override inheritance and biological givenness. Consider the great popularity of "extreme makeovers" in which people's organs and features are reconstructed so that they can appear more healthy or beautiful. Add to this the potential for external adornment through clothing and accessories—all with the intention of constructing a more fashionable identity—and we have the perfect display of a consumer society. Who I am is what I can afford.

When discussing the evils of consumerism, it is important to underscore that consumption itself is not the problem. We all need to ingest food, drink water, and purchase the goods that make life possible. What is problematic is the reduction of life's elements to commodities that can be bought and sold. When something is simply a commodity, it has been turned into an object shorn of connections to others. When we treat food as a mere commodity, for instance, we do not need to worry about whether the soil in which it was grown is healthy and vibrant, whether the water that nurtured it is in plentiful and clean supply, or whether the workers who produced and processed it were fairly compensated and justly treated. It is reduced to fuel. It ceases to be a natural, cultural, and spiritual product made possible by a great array of geochemical, biological, social, and religious relationships. When food is reduced to a commodity, these relationships are not acknowledged or honored. As a result, they are more open to harm and destruction.

We develop a deep understanding of, and thus appreciation for, our relationships with others primarily as we directly engage and work closely with the sources of life. This means that we need to be as actively and practically involved in the maintenance of these relationships as we can. We need to get in closer touch with family members, friends, our bodies, and biophysical processes, so that at the first moment of distress we can begin the work of repair and restoration. A consumerist lifestyle, owing to its passive nature, makes this virtually impossible. As consumers we are mostly ignorant of what it takes to build healthy relationships, strong families, vibrant communities, and flourishing natural habitats. We are trained away from expending attention and effort on protecting and nurturing the sources of life and are taught that what we need is purchasable with the ease of a credit-card swipe.

Ignorance is one of the most destructive side effects of a consumerist society, particularly from the perspective of the promotion of delight. If we remember that the practice of delight is reflected in our ability to praise and thank God, then it is of the greatest importance that we know and understand what we are grateful for and why God is praiseworthy. In a significant respect, the possibility of authentic gratitude simply depends on our knowledge and understanding, for without them our words of thanks are either abstract or hollow. Consider partaking of a meal. When we know and appreciate the many factors that contributed to the meal's success—a cook who cared enough about us to plan and make it, healthy plant and animal life, vibrant farming communities, good weather, healthy bodies that can enjoy the taste of good food—we gain a sense of the costliness and goodness of what is set before us. But when we eat in ignorance—and most of us do this most of the time—any gratitude we can muster is abstract. We can't really be grateful because we don't know all that we are to be grateful for.

If we are to be truly grateful and thus capable of the praise God deserves, we need to learn to count honestly and fully the costs of our living. A consumer society makes this increasingly difficult to do. Virtually all we know about what we want to consume is its sale price. We don't know the costs—material, ecological, social—that went into the making of any commodity. Nor do we much appreciate the effects of our consumption. Our waste simply goes to the curb, where it will be handled by sanitation professionals. Consumerism, in short, turns us into ignorant and irresponsible people who are unable to appreciate and appropriately respond to the great variety and amount of gifts lavishly given to us every day. We have become blind to the grace of God at work all around us. If we were not so blind, we would be able to join in the Nishmat prayer often recited by observant Jews at the close of their Sabbath celebration:

> Were our mouths filled with song as the sea,
> Our tongues with melody as the multitude of its waves,
> Our lips with praise as the expanse of the heavens,
> Our eyes bright as the sun and the moon,
> Our hands spread out as the eagles of the heaven,
> Our feet swift as the deer,
> We would still be unable to adequately acknowledge You and bless
>   Your name,
> O Lord our God and God of our fathers,
> For even one thousand-thousand-myriad-myriad part of the favors
> You have bestowed upon our fathers and upon us . . .[6]

The more we appreciate and engage creation in its depth and variety, the greater, and the more spontaneous and natural, will be our gratitude and praise.

The success of consumerism is heavily dependent on creating confusion about needs and wants. As has long been observed, the triumph of consumerism as the world's leading ideology in the last century has everything to do with creating insecure and ungrateful consumers, people who do not appreciate what really is valuable and important in life. Because we are ignorant about the true requirements of life and the wealth of memberships that nurture it along the way, we are readily convinced that products can substitute for relationships. In the absence of relationships that feed and inspire us, we turn to products to fill the void. When the void becomes large enough, there is simply no limit to the number of products we "need" to make our lives whole or a joy. Life becomes an endless shopping trip for happiness.

Obviously this is not the whole story behind consumerism. Historians like Gary Cross have done an excellent job of showing us how in the last century the purchase of consumer items was as much about constructing social identities, overcoming ethnic differences, and participating in mass democratic processes, as it was about accumulating stuff. Consumerism, in this context at least, gave diverse people the opportunity to appear to be on an equal footing with others. Through the purchase of goods the rhetoric of liberty and democracy took on concrete forms as people simultaneously expressed themselves while sharing in the mass ownership of products.[7]

But at this point an important question emerges: what sort of identity is constructed in a world of consumerism? Given that the world of consumerism is heavily influenced by the vagaries of marketing and fashion, it is hard to see how the identities we purchase are in any meaningful way conducive to personal, social, or ecological well-being. Do these identities promote the introspection that would encourage us to highlight, honor, and celebrate our interdependence with others? Far from affirming and helping us nurture our relationships, our consumer society produces heightened, highly stylized forms of individualism.

Expressive individualism is thus the ideal context in which the mode of life as *appearing* can take hold. Here what matters about the products we buy is not their use value but their sign value. We do not buy a car simply for the purpose of getting us from one place to another. Rather, we buy a particular make or style of car so that in driving it we will project a desired image. I don't actually have to be an outdoorsman or a Hollywood starlet to participate in the look by driving a four-wheel-drive sport utility vehicle or a convertible roadster. What has happened here is the elevation of the sign, image, or style above reality or substance.

Given suitable attire and props (and funds!), we can share in the look of any identity without participating in the discipline of relationships that would make it real. We live in what the French theorist Guy Debord called the "society of the spectacle."

In this society people are increasingly passive, alone, and bewildered as they wait to be lured into purchasing and consuming a meaning context or a world constructed by someone else. Personal identities are not forged through patient work to understand and appreciate the many layers of relationship that in fact feed into our living. Instead, they are selected from myriad options made available to us by image and brand consultants and by advertising campaigns. The range of options, we can be assured, will ever increase, for marketing success and thus corporate profit depend on our being willing to change our identity to suit the current fashion.

The society of the spectacle, we can now see, does not simply operate on the surface level of appearances: it aims to take hold of our lives at the level of our fundamental desires. It transforms at the most basic level what we understand the world to be. Steven Best and Douglas Kellner have usefully summarized this situation as follows: "The spectacle escalates abstraction to the point where one no longer lives in the world per se . . . but in an abstract *image* of the world."[8] Though we may be entertained by someone's image of a world, it is hard to think that an *image* of the world, particularly one that is geared to increasing someone else's profitability, could ever be the source of abiding delight.

This last point represents the climax of a process that I have been charting in the movement from *being* to *having* to *appearing*. Modern and postmodern culture has gone a long way toward destroying our experience of the world as God's creation. Rather than understanding and engaging each other and our natural home as concrete manifestations of the love and care of God, we have come to handle reality as it is packaged and presented to us by professional elites, technicians, institutions, market-ers, and image consultants. What is lost is not simply our hold on reality as a deep, varied set of relationships that feed into and inspire our being. Also lost is our capacity to delight in and show gratitude and praise for the many blessings that make our life possible and a joy.

According to postmodernists like Jean Baudrillard, we are in a cultural situation where we, as trained consumers, can no longer distinguish be-tween reality and illusion. We are so caught up in the worlds of consump-tion and commodification, the spectacle and the political language of spin, that we no longer know who we are, where we are, and how our living is made possible. This practical and in some senses staged or planned confusion has not only led directly to the loss of meaning or purpose in much of contemporary North American life. It has significantly impaired our capacity for joy. Our confusion has made it much less likely that we will find in our experience or activity the gifts and the grace of God that we can unqualifiedly affirm or over which pronounce an "amen."

Especially in a time of widely professed belief in God, we need to acknowledge that the patterns of our dominant culture pronounce and encourage practical atheism. In a time of practical atheism people are cut off from deep relationships with others, which means that we are cut off from God's life-giving and life-sustaining ways at work in those relationships. Having lost our contact with God, we turn to religious beliefs or pious sentiments that are forced, hollow, or merely ornamental. Though we desperately search for moments of peace and joy, we do not find them, for the structures of our living keep us trapped within a graceless world of our own or someone else's devising.

6

Pain and Suffering

■ It is difficult to imagine a more serious impediment to the practice of delight than our experience of pain and suffering in the world. When children are born with horribly debilitating diseases, or communities are destroyed by war, famine, fire, or earthquake, or when we consider the massive suffering in animal species that is simply part of evolutionary development, it is natural to conclude that any and all delight is finally a sham. God, on this view, does not deserve our praise and thanksgiving, for the world appears to be deeply flawed, too susceptible to merciless chance. Rather than bearing witness to God's abiding love and concern, we are tempted to concede that we live in a cold, random, and meaningless universe. Our experience of misery and death suggests a nonexistent, absent, or tyrannical God. There is no *menuha*, we might say, because the chaos that threatened creation from the beginning has overtaken God's (and our own) hopes for peace and joy.

When we are talking about pain and suffering, it is crucial that we not try to explain it away or presume to understand what is finally a mystery. In important respects, we have to admit that we do not comprehend God's ways with the world. So we need to be very attentive to the presuppositions that frame our understanding and concerns. For instance, should we even characterize the issue as a "problem" that falls within the scope of what has come to be called "theodicy"? According to this tradition of thought, evil and suffering are so problematic because they cannot be reconciled with a loving and all-powerful God. If God loves us, the abundance of evil suggests that God is powerless to do much about it, whereas if God is all-powerful, the presence of so much suffering indicates that God doesn't really care. Given these two options, many opt for a less powerful, though certainly nice and well-meaning, God.

A third option, one more frequently taken in the period of modernity, is to dispense with the idea of God altogether. On this atheistic view, there is simply too much pain and suffering in the world to warrant any belief in God whatsoever. Consider the words of the nineteenth-century philosopher Arthur Schopenhauer:

> The shortness of life, so often lamented, may be perhaps the very best thing about it. If, finally, we were to bring to the sight of everyone the terrible sufferings and afflictions to which his life is constantly exposed, he would be seized with horror. If we were to conduct the most hardened and cal-loused optimist through hospitals, infirmaries, operating theaters, through prisons, torture-chambers, and slave hovels, over battlefields and to places of execution; if we were to open to him all the dark abodes of misery, where it shuns the gaze of cold curiosity, and finally were to allow him to glance into the dungeons of Ugolino where prisoners starved to death, he too would certainly see in the end what kind of world is this *meilleur des mondes possibles* [best of all possible worlds]. For whence did Dante get the material for his hell, if not from this actual world of ours?[1]

Moreover, the range of suffering is not confined to human beings. The animal world too is shot through with so much pain and seemingly senseless death—vicious forms of predation, the recurrence of mass starvation among species—that Charles Darwin, who began his scientific career with a rather traditional belief in God as the Creator of all, came to doubt the compatibility of such belief with the seeming wastage and brutality of natural selection. The problem for him was not simply nature's randomness but that "the suffering of millions of the lower animals throughout almost endless time," as well as the death of his ten-year-old daughter Annie, could not be reconciled with the idea of a benevolent deity.

For both Schopenhauer and Darwin, having presupposed that a theodicy approach is the correct way to frame the issue, the evidence of so much pain and suffering compelled them to characterize evolutionary processes as fundamentally meaningless, random, and without ultimate purpose. But surely this is a curious result, particularly when we remember that the experience of suffering was hardly foreign to the biblical writers who gave us the rationale for Sabbath delight in the first place. The psalms, for instance, reverberate with themes of abandonment, loss, misery, and shame:

For my soul is full of troubles,
    and my life draws near to Sheol.
I am counted among those who go down to the Pit;
    I am like those who have no help,
like those forsaken among the dead,
    like the slain that lie in the grave,
like those whom you remember no more,
    for they are cut off from your hand.
You have put me in the depths of the Pit,
    in the regions dark and deep.

(Ps. 88:3–6)

Moreover, the histories of the Israelites and the early Christians were punctuated with the suffering of deprivation, slavery, exile, persecution, and martyrdom. For them, pain and suffering, while clearly a concern to be faced and handled, were not the occasion to abandon trust or forsake hope. They were instead moments—sometimes very difficult—when God's people's characterizations of God and creation could be made more honest, their devotion and care more merciful and true.

What changed so that in one instance we have the rejection of God and in the other a tenacious holding on to God ("In the day of my trouble I will call on you, for you will answer me," Ps. 86:7)? One way to understand this shift is to say that the theodicy approach to pain and suffering was flawed from the start. Theodicy in its classical formulation in the seventeenth and eighteenth centuries developed at precisely the same time as the world ceased to be understood as God's creation, when reality came to be understood as a mechanism that can be modified and manipulated to suit human designs. God is practically absent from this world—or perhaps more accurately, the god that remains is one that will underwrite or legitimate the aims we choose for ourselves—while human ingenuity and power take center stage. The power we want, and thus the sort of power we project upon God, is of the sort that eliminates all contingency and finitude and thus also all pain and suffering. Since we like to think of ourselves as autonomous, self-subsisting beings having no need of others, we come to think of God in similar invulnerable terms. God and suffering are seen as mutually exclusive.

The biblical God not only suffers with us in covenant relationship but also, with the incarnation of Jesus Christ, enters into our bodily pain and death. Indeed, it is through Christ's personal suffering that we are invited into the depths of God's own life. When we believe that suffering and God are incompatible, what we have really done is elevate our own idolatrous interests, desires, fears, and worries above an honest accounting for the depth and mystery of life and the limits of human power and striving. Pain and suffering should not be cast as "problems" that need to be "explained" or "solved," eliminated because they represent an affront to the world we would choose or make for ourselves. In fact, it is a mistake to look for a "solution," since this becomes an excuse to avoid the communal disciplines of care and constancy that enable us together to bear, absorb, and grow through each other's hurt.

Facing and Naming the Pain

Given this brief examination of theodicy's problematic way of putting the issue, it is clear that we need to be very careful about the ways we name and characterize suffering. Suffering does not happen in the abstract, nor is it universally felt at all times in the same way. We need to be honest and as precise as possible with our words, acknowledging that people occupy particular histories and traditions.

Especially in an era of individualism, we are readily tempted to reduce suffering to whatever impedes our freedom or brings us displeasure and discomfort. Think here of the common complaint that life does not go as we planned or expected. It is easy to interpret events as evil or to claim that the world we live in is rigged against our personal success. But is it really? The problem with this anthropocentric, even egocentric approach is that it assumes that the whole of reality should be geared to the satisfaction of our narrow wishes. This assumption is deeply at odds with the creation narrative that proclaims God's *menuha* as creation's ultimate goal, and with the experience of Job, who learns through his pain and suffering that the goods of this world are not tailored to his interests and that the scope of God's concern extends far beyond humanity to include all of creation. Our best efforts to establish an accountant's ledger of good and evil will often miss the mark.

We also need to be careful that the naming of our experiences not be a masked form of disdain for this world or contempt for this life. Friedrich Nietzsche argued persuasively that much of our philosophizing and theologizing amount to inventions of ideal, supernatural realms so that we despise and seek to rise above the world as we commonly or naturally experience it. Philosophers and theologians, on this view, construct abstract otherworldly realities—Plato's perfect, eternal "Forms," Gnostic Christianity's heavenly bliss—and then argue that these, rather than earthly, changeable experience, are what life is all about. Too much of our thinking, Nietzsche maintained, amounts to a justification of our yen to escape from or condemn this life. Why do we want escape? Because life is difficult and punctuated with pain. So rather than face life honestly as it really is, we prefer to flee it and then from the realm of an imagined paradise pronounce a negative judgment upon it. This flight mechanism Nietzsche characterized as the height of decadence, because it is a symptom of life's decline, a testimony to our unwillingness to affirm life in all its dimensions and trajectories. What Nietzsche understood so well is that in the face of pain and suffering our temptation is to turn away, to reject reality as not good enough or not in proper alignment with what we want or expect.[2] Clearly, however, rejection cannot be the basis for the practice of delight, particularly when we remember that our delighting in creation presupposes a robust affirmation of it.

If we want to speak more honestly about pain and suffering, we need a broader perspective, one that takes us beyond our presumed understanding, fears, resentment, disappointment, and narrow interests. The customary ways we have of conceiving and ordering our world are shot through with forms of violence that exacerbate our collective suffering. We do not appreciate well enough how much of the pain and suffering in our lives is attributable to the cultural patterns or mechanisms we use to establish what we think a "good" life is. A significant amount of the misery that afflicts us is the effect of our sometimes tragically mistaken "best efforts" to succeed in life.

It is not enough to argue, as many have, that much human suffering is the result of bad or immoral choices people make. On this view, decisions that either directly or indirectly harm others are the result of human freedom run amok. The presupposition is that if we get freedom right, then the suffering that was produced by our bad choices will finally go away. But what if our freedom, tragically malformed as it often is—think of people caught up in cycles of violent or sexual abuse, the hordes of children weaned on the violence and egomania of television and computer games—is not something we can get right on our own? This is the crucial question that Sabbath teaching and the doctrine of creation are uniquely suited to address.

Sabbath discipline fosters in us an appreciation for creation as God sees it. We cannot acquire this divine point of view on our own. We need our freedom to be properly inspired and formed, and for this formation we need to depend on God. The Hebrews had to learn this dependence in a humbling journey: forty years in the wilderness relying on God for direction and for the satisfaction of their every need. This wandering wilderness experience was necessary so that the emerging people of God would not think that culture is the effect or product of merely human decision and design. During their wandering, the Hebrews could think seriously about the inspiration and means behind Egyptian culture. They could remember that Egypt, for all its glory and success, was a site of oppression and violence, the forced subjugation and misery of hordes of people for the benefit of a few. In direct contrast to the Egyptians, the Hebrews would be called out to form a society and nation that was no longer premised on violence and inflicted suffering. Primarily through their Sabbath teaching, they were to be inspired by God's ways of justice, joy, and peace. Of course it would take generations and multiple prophetic voices for them to see and then work to root out even minimally the violence within their own midst. In the end, God's ways of ordering reality are fundamentally at odds with our own.

Violence and the Cross

To understand this point, we need to think more carefully about how violence enters into and shapes the heart of human culture. The ideas of mimetic theory, particularly as they have been expounded by René Girard and James Alison, are especially helpful in this regard, because they emphasize the relation between our dependence upon and need for one another and the formation of personal identity and desire. According to this view, we develop ourselves as persons by imitating others. Our imitation takes many forms, as when we copy speech patterns or mimic behaviors, but its most far-reaching dimension occurs on the level of desire. Who we are and what we want in life come to be defined by what others possess and have become. Our identity is thus dependent on the identity of others. This dependence, which is quite natural and creaturely, becomes the basis for serious conflict as people fail or refuse to acknowledge it properly. The problem is that we like to think that our desire is original with us; no one likes to be told that in their efforts to forge an identity they are merely copying or imitating (from the Greek word *mimesis*) someone else. To admit that we are "copycats" would be to affirm that we need each other and could not get along well without others. Given our prideful propensities and our desire to be self-standing, autonomous beings—Adam and Eve preferred to be gods themselves rather than live by the generosity and grace of God—this is not an admission we care to make. Our refusal amounts to a denial of interdependence.

As we come into conflict with others, precisely by denying our dependence upon (and rivalry with) them, a handy strategy is to find someone else to blame for our quarrels. Imagine that Bill wants to be an exceptional athlete like Carl. At first Carl is flattered by Bill's admiration and may even help Bill by allowing him to train alongside. But then Bill slowly surpasses Carl in skill, and an intense rivalry, perhaps even hatred, develops between them. Rather than expressing appreciation to Carl for his inspiration and support, Bill claims he is a superior athlete and attained his superior status through inborn talent and hard work. Carl, on the other hand, has become intensely jealous and cannot acknowledge that Bill has compelled him to become a better athlete than he once was. Now locked in their animus toward each other, they sense that the only way to patch things up and salvage their fragile relation is to vent their anger at someone else, a foreign competitor perhaps, who can become the source of their anger or frustration. Any peace Bill and Carl can enjoy will thus be at the expense of another.

According to mimetic theory, the only peace our society offers is made possible by the demonizing or scapegoating of someone who is declared to be responsible for our conflicts. We have a cultural and personal need to victimize, banish, or even kill others so that we can deal with the rivalry that invariably creeps into our relations due to our dependence on one another. This is a false and unenduring peace, however, because it never addresses the rivalry and envy that set the victimization and demonization going in the first place. Still, the key institutions of culture, ranging from education to politics to religion, sanction and require this violent scapegoating. Cultural success, in other words, is premised on the violent oppression of others. Since the time of Cain, society has been rooted in murder.

Clearly, with this violent underpinning, we should expect that a great deal of misery comes to us as the effect of our own hand. Our refusal to acknowledge the many layers of interdependence that make life possible put us in contexts of intractable and painful struggle. The problem is that we don't see it this way. We are so caught up in structures of self-deception and self-importance that if we are to see our violence and self-delusion for what they really are, God must point it out to us.

This, say Girard and Alison, is what happens on the cross. Jesus Christ is revealed to us as the innocent victim, and in his innocence we see for the first time the extent of our contentious, envious, murderous ways. Sin is the blindness in us that compels us to see our violent ways as good. To gain a true vision of the full extent of our violence so that we can be helped to correct it, we need the light of the resurrection to shine on us. It is in light of the forgiveness made possible by the cross that we see our sinfulness aright for the first time.

The coming of Christ, and the founding of the church as Christ's continuing presence among us, is an event of immense proportions. It means, says Alison, "the undoing of the whole social structure of the world, which is ultimately futile, because it is, to its very roots, self-destructive and based on self-destruction."[3] Christ makes possible the correction of personal desire so that we can form our identities in nonrivalrous ways, aware that we all live by the grace of God and the gifts of each other. "God's love for us is the love by which Jesus was empowered *as a human being* to create for us—which means to understand and imagine and invent for us—a way out of our violence and death."[4] Christ, through the church, makes possible a new kind of social existence in which our interdependence, rather than being the occasion for conflict, is strengthened through mutual upbuilding and support. The apostle Paul puts this beautifully in his second letter to the Corinthians (5:17–18): "So if anyone is in Christ, there is a new creation: everything old has passed away; see, everything has become new! All this is from God, who reconciled us to himself through Christ, and has given us the ministry of reconciliation."

Human life no longer needs to be lived under the perennial regime of sin and violence. Christ's resurrection, as the revelation and overcoming of our death-wielding ways, makes possible a new kind of life, restoring creation to its original intent of participating in God's own life of joy, peace, and *menuha*. The resurrection, in short, helps us know what creation is ultimately about as a forgiven and reconciled existence formed in grateful acceptance of gift upon gift.

Christ's opening up of a new, nonviolent life is best understood in a Sabbath context, since it is one of the key elements of Sabbath teaching that we do not live by our own might or cunning (since this is a path built upon violence) but through the nurture of others and the grace of God. This humbling realization enables authentic thanksgiving and praise. It is also the basis upon which to build practices of forgiveness and reconciliation. Once we learn to appreciate our own lives and those around us as gifts from God, we do not need to enter into bitter struggle and inflict various forms of pain and suffering upon each other. The many relations that feed into our being and literally constitute it can now be embraced and celebrated as so many forms of manna from heaven.

The Christian response to pain and suffering is always a bodily response. I mean "bodily" in two senses: first, as a response that takes seriously our lives as biological, embodied beings, and second, as a response that assumes our living within a social body. For Christians there can be no escape from or condemnation of material reality, because this approach amounts to a gnostic denial of the incarnate life of God. God lives among us and has entered fully into our life's bodily suffering and joy. We have no right to expect a painless life, because Christ himself did not. This realization, however, does not mean that we are to seek out pain in the belief that pain is a good in itself or serves an always noble purpose. In many instances we will find no nobility in it at all. What we need are ways to express appropriate rage and bewilderment while staying faithful to the world as God made it. In times like this we need the wisdom of the lament, which Stanley Hauerwas has helpfully described as "the cry of protest schooled by our faith in a God who would have us serve the world by exposing its false comforts and deceptions."[5]

It would be dishonest and arrogant to assume that life should be without suffering. It would be idolatrous to shift the problem of our suffering to God by turning God into a mere "explanation" for our troubles. What we are called to do, and in this calling we have the example of Christ to follow, is practice forms of compassion that do not avoid pain and suffering but bind them up within a community of care.

Given the social and relational character of the Christian's response to pain and suffering, Joel Shuman is correct when he observes that community is a more fundamental ontological category than biology.[6] What he means by this is that who we are as Christians, our very identity, is defined by our participation in a larger social body we call the church. We never face our suffering alone but as members of the body of Christ trained in discipleship to be attentive to each other's needs and present to each other in times of pain and suffering. If we are to bear each other's burdens, as the gospel clearly teaches, then we must learn to be available to each other, recognizing that in this availability we become gifts to each other. To live in the body of Christ is to expose the lie that we are self-sufficient beings. Through the body we are strengthened and carried by a divine power and mercy greater than anything we could ever experience on our own. The care of the social body, even more so than the proper functioning of our material body, is what finally makes us whole. The body of Christ tells us that we are gifts to each other, rather than rivals, and once we appreciate this cruciform but also Sabbath reality, we are freed to enter life's possibilities with mercy, confidence, and the assurance of abundance.

Many of us, however, find it difficult to accept our need and the gifts of those who seek to help us. We prefer to be self-reliant, believing that admitting need is a sign of personal weakness and failure. The body of Christ must confront this sentiment head on as antithetical to the ways of God and creation. To be a creature is, by definition, to be in need of concrete support and nurture in biological, social, and divine contexts. We need to appreciate, as Hauerwas has noted, that "our neediness is also the source of our greatest strength, for our need requires the cooperation and love of others from which derives our ability not only to live but to flourish."[7] As we come to see that we are all patients and beggars before God and each other, perhaps we will develop the attention and patience to be servants worthy of the calling of Christ.

The Suffering of Creation

Our discussion about cultural violence and human sinfulness has been important because these play a major role in producing pain and suffering. What Alison refers to as "the snarling up of creation" is in many cases the effect of our rivalry, arrogance, and ingratitude. But does human violence account for all the suffering we see in creation, and is it responsible for all our pain? Questioning of this sort has prompted some theologians and philosophers to distinguish moral and natural evil (we should remember, however, that "nature" is not a biblical but a secular category). While "moral evils" follow from the abuse or distortion of human freedom, "natural evils" like disease, ecological or meteorological disasters, and (nonviolent) death do not.

Once again, it is very important that we be careful with our naming, since it is not clear how precisely or neatly the line between moral and natural evil can be drawn. We are becoming aware that the effects of human activity have a far wider and longer reach than we had previously believed. The human invention of tens of thousands of never-before-seen poisons and toxins, our production of greenhouse gases through the unprecedented burning of fossil fuels, the massive alteration of the earth's topography through agriculture, urbanization, coastal development, deforestation, desertification, and the draining of wetlands, plus the rapid acceleration of species extinction and habitat loss, mean that we no longer know what is a "natural" event or effect. It is quite likely, though virtually impossible to prove without doubt, that our drive to cultural and personal success, expressed in the destructive means just mentioned, has meant an increase and invention of many new forms of disease, disaster, and unnecessary death. What at first glance appears to be a natural evil (a village-destroying mudslide) may actually be a moral evil (the effect of irresponsible, profit-driven hillside deforestation). When we conceive health and flourishing in holistic terms, we realize that our bodies thrive in sympathetic concert with many other natural bodies. We can no longer assume that our minds and bodies will function well if we have exhausted, poisoned, or destroyed the natural contexts they depend upon.

Even so, it does make sense to say that not all suffering is the direct result of human activity. Some of it follows from the normal and to be expected (if not welcomed) ordering of the world. Earthquakes and volcanoes, tornadoes and hurricanes, and even various forms of disease are geophysical and physiological events that indicate a dynamic and changeable world. It depends on one's point of view, since (to take one example) the phenomenon of tectonic shift that gives us earthquakes also gave us the Rockies and the geologic uplift necessary for a diverse biosphere. Could we adapt to varying biological conditions if we never experienced pain of any kind?

Suggesting that some suffering is simply inescapable does not mean that creation is evil or in itself deficient; it is, rather, following the course that in its widest scope is conducive to the continuation and development of more life. The suffering in creation is not to be explained away. Our task is to learn to bear it together.

This conclusion is easier stated than lived. Consider the situation of Frances Young, a British theologian, and her son Arthur. Arthur was born brain-damaged due to a small placenta. His life, as well as the lives of those who love and support him, has been a daily struggle with grief and frustration, since Arthur cannot accomplish the most basic tasks many of us take for granted. How does one deal with the suffering that is Arthur's life or with the pain of those who care for him? What we learn from Young is striking and difficult, for in her book *Face to Face* she recounts how worshiping and joining with a Christian community in an area of social deprivation helped her understand our collective vulnerability and our need for relationship and mutual help. Worship, that most concrete expression of Sabbath discipline that trains us to focus on the grace of God in our midst, became the means for her to overcome the despair or anger that otherwise could have consumed her.

The movement toward worship was hardly easy. Stress, guilt, fatigue, self-pity, embarrassment, frustration, obsession—these are the daily accompaniments of chronic, debilitating disease. But as Young shows, these griefs can be borne within a worshiping community that welcomes and cares without fear or judgment for others no matter who, or how healthy or "normal," they are. In an important sense, what Young is describing here is the concrete realization of the Sabbath notion that creation, because of its strengthening and grace-filled networks of relationship, is to be affirmed and loved and celebrated even in the midst of its pain and disfigurement. She asks a question that is really the most vital: "Might not the real triumph be the ability to receive from one another, to discover interdependence, to find values which make success and death equally irrelevant?"[8]

Young shows us through her story that pain and suffering are not to be denied or shunned but rather "accepted" as vital ingredients of the life of faith. When we learn to accept and bear our pain together, we develop the habits that best equip us to build communities that acknowledge and celebrate our need for each other. When we fully and without rivalry welcome others, even those who seemingly do not have much to offer in return, we recognize our interdependence and learn the arts of sharing, forgiveness, and gratitude. Young again puts it best:

> The key, it seems to me, is in establishing a reciprocal relationship with the handicapped. The most fundamental aspect of this is the recognition, not that we are doing them good, but that they are doing something for us. The thing that finally resolved my distress was the discovery that I had to give thanks for Arthur. It was no longer a case of accepting him, but rejoicing in him and receiving from him . . . It is with him that I find the fruits of the Spirit: love, joy, peace, patience, kindness, goodness, faithfulness, humility and self-control.[9]

While Young's story is helpful for dealing with nonviolent human pain and suffering, the question still remains: how are we to understand the massive amount of nonhuman pain and suffering we see in creation? This question is important because of God's intention that *menuha* be enjoyed by the whole creation. We must not predicate our delight on the misery or exhaustion of our nonhuman neighbors.

Our question about nonhuman suffering becomes urgent when we recognize that evolutionary processes presuppose struggle and death. As organisms have developed and adapted to changing environmental conditions, millions of members and species have simply gone extinct. Moreover, the means of species' success often entail forms of predation that we would consider cruel and sometimes wasteful. Must killer whales play with (torture?) half-alive, mutilated seals before they finally eat them? It is hard for us to imagine this scenario as giving rise to anyone's delight, especially not God's.

As we search for an adequate response to this difficult reality, we do well to heed God's warning that came to Job from out of the whirlwind advising us that we not darken any counsel with "words without knowledge" (Job 38:2). Regarding the complexity of ecological functioning, there is so much that we simply do not see or know. And regarding what this functioning *means* we know even less. The barrage of questions God fires at Job has the effect of destabilizing the certainties we think we can take for granted. Is predation an evil and unnecessary form of food procurement? Job learns that God is fully aware that predation occurs. Indeed, the existence of Behemoth suggests that God made a creature so strong and frightful (violent?) that only God can approach it with a "sword" so as to restrain it (40:15–24). Leviathan represents an equally ferocious creature that we would do our best to leave alone. Yet God finds a reason to delight in creatures such as these: "I will not keep silence concerning its limbs, or its mighty strength, or its splendid frame" (41:12).

Whether these creatures are mythic or real, it is clear that the text of Job aims to teach us that we must not reduce the broad, deep sweep of creation to a narrowly human plane. We cannot fully comprehend the purposes of God. The suffering and pain that follow from the ferocity of creatures may play a more important role in the overall health of species and habitats than we can appreciate. Struggle in nature may be one of the means through which species, and with them the whole of creation, are strengthened. Of course, not all of nature is "red in tooth and claw," since natural processes entail cooperation as well as competition. But from the perspective of pain and suffering, we may be well advised to acknowledge that animal suffering, though not always apparently so, may be part of a more inclusive good.

We need to be careful not to impose our sense of a just world on God. Though we have great difficulty understanding phenomena of death and struggle—why it happens and when, or why it occurs to the degree that it does—the fact of the matter is that life depends upon it. Were soil to be devoid of all death and struggle—particularly at the microbial and microorganism levels—it could no longer sustain vegetative and animal life. Soil that is without death is sterile, literally dead. It needs death to be "alive." From this soil perspective we can say that the life of some simply depends on the death of others.

Is this how life will always be? Of course this is a difficult question to answer. Scripture gives us a suggestive glimpse of another possibility when Moses encounters God in the burning bush that is not consumed. Perhaps when we more fully enter into the life of God we will experience the power of life that does not destroy or consume but always and only gives life and light.

In the meantime, our response to suffering and pain, even when it involves our nonhuman neighbors, is not to deny or turn away from it. Nor is it to "solve" it, since solving is not within our comprehension or power. What we need to learn is the honest, patient attentiveness that will enable us to be more merciful members of God's creation. Our task is to be transformed by the suffering of God himself, and then from the perspective of this transformation welcome the whole creation with humility, care, gratitude, and the overall aim of celebration. Above all we need to remember that our celebration is only in its beginning phase. In part this is because the transformation begun in us through Christ is not yet complete. As Alison puts it, "It is exactly our hope in God's creative vivaciousness which allows us *not* to grasp onto our [violent] story, but to allow God to create, by means of us, something much richer and more extraordinary than we could imagine we are about."[10]

Hope is a rupture in the systems of violence and suffering: it holds before us possibilities that are genuinely new and welcoming of life. It lets us know that we are not condemned to repeat over and over again our destructive past. Hope makes it possible for us to sing and rejoice even in the midst of our pain, because hope opens our being and our imagination so that we can find comfort and support in the relationships that carry and sustain us through all of life's trials and joys. Hope is not to be confused with an optimism we nurture in ourselves; rather it is strength and vision we draw from our dependence upon and celebration of others. This is our Sabbath discipline: to be trained in the strengthening and celebration of relationships—our life together.

Part 2

The Sabbath
in Practical Context

7

Work and the Sabbath

■ The close association between Sabbath and rest easily leads us to believe that Sabbath observance is somehow the opposite of work, or that the Sabbath has to do with a leisurely or narrowly defined religious domain entirely different or separate from the world of labor and daily business. On this view, work has its own sphere of influence, its own set of objectives and manners, while the Sabbath runs according to a very different schedule and set of priorities. This neat bifurcation between work life and Sabbath life needs to be challenged, since it encourages a false, soul-damaging division between religious and mundane existence, between what we do on Sundays and what we do the rest of the week.

While it would be a mistake to collapse work and the Sabbath into one another—they are clearly not the same—it is no less an error to think that these two spheres or dimensions of life do not inform each other. Sabbath observance, if it is to be true and not a sham, must necessarily extend into and be completed, made concrete, in our work lives. Conversely, without certain kinds of work, work that contributes to the good of each other, genuine rest and delight become highly unlikely, if not impossible. Just as the Sabbath can inform the way we work and the kinds of work we perform by giving it a particular focus and objective, so too will our work affect and define the kinds of Sabbath we can enjoy. For example, a soul daily degraded by inhumane or destructive work cannot simply will itself to authentic praise and delight.

Thinking this way requires that we first overcome a long history of interpretation that views work as an evil, an inescapable bane on human existence. This view, which often has in mind the curse given to Eve and then Adam in Genesis 3:16–19 ("in pain you shall bring forth children . . . in toil you shall eat . . . by the sweat of your face you shall eat bread"), assumes that work is a result of divine punishment and proposes that human life would be better without it. It is difficult to know, however, what a nonworking *human* life would be or what, practically speaking, such a world would look like, since work (which is not to be identified with "wage labor") simply is the practical context through which we develop ourselves as individuals and as social beings. Productive work is essential and vital, for through it life is maintained and developed into a meaningful and satisfying world. No doubt certain kinds of work—work that is pure drudgery or monotony, work that is degrading, destructive, and violent—are indeed a curse. But the problem is not work itself but rather an economy that is infected by sinfulness and that as a result grossly distorts the work on which it depends.

Work and Salvation

Arguing for the value of work does not mean that through work we will somehow accomplish our salvation. Salvation is always a gift of God that we receive by participation. The meaning of this participation becomes more apparent in the light of my earlier discussion of the connection between health, wholeness, and salvation. Our temptation is to view salvation as a discrete package, passively received, that is an add-on to the end of life. This picture is not true to the gospel portrayal of salvation made incarnate in the flesh of Jesus Christ. Here we see that salvation is the restoration and strengthening of souls and bodies. It is a process that is worked out in the intimacy of our hearts and revealed in the transformation of our mundane daily lives. Though we do not, indeed cannot, initiate this process of healing and wholeness—it remains forever a gift—we do need to engage in actions that foster and celebrate God's life-giving power within and among us. As the letter of James reminds us, faith withers and dies when it is not realized and made incarnate in the Christ-inspired work of feeding, healing, building, teaching, restoring, and serving. Our participation in the ways of salvation inevitably calls us to attend to and address the illness and brokenness around us, since we cannot be fully well if the social and biological communities that enable our well-being are languishing or in distress. Salvation does not exist in otherworldly isolation, nor is it a private possession that we can safely bury in the ground for later use. It follows from and builds upon creation as its restoring and reconciling action.

When we characterize human activity this broadly in terms of the drama of salvation, it is easier to appreciate why human work is so significant: it enables us to figure out and know our place in the world and to develop ourselves as creatures responsibly placed within God's creation. Work enables us to participate in the sustaining and saving work of God that goes on all around us. When we work, what we are really doing is responding to the grace of God evident in our families, communities, and natural habitats. *Grace*, in its most fundamental meaning, refers to God's self-involvement in and dedication to the whole creation to see that it is healthy and whole. When we respond to this grace, we also dedicate ourselves to the goal of supporting and strengthening our social and natural homes. This is our universal calling: to serve and keep God's creation (Gen. 2:15). Human work, in all its diverse forms, is at its best when it follows from this divinely appointed vocation.

It is important to distinguish vocation from career, not because careers are inherently evil but because they often lack the inspiration and direction of a larger social and divine purpose. A career is an occupation we hope will bring the greatest amount of personal satisfaction and benefit. Given that what personally satisfies can change, especially due to economic pressure or changing marketing messages, many people will try—or, through factory closings, corporate downsizing, personal debt, or endemic unemployment, be forced to move into—several different careers in the course of their work life. Careers and the work performed under their umbrella often lack a clear sense that we as workers are responding to, participating in, and contributing to the love of God made manifest in the divine work of creation. When work is reduced to careerism, its divine dimension and intention are cut off. The inevitable consequence is the distortion of humanity and creation.

The way we think about work, and thus the kinds of work we encourage and accept, always presupposes a set of beliefs about what it is to be a person. If we consider people primarily as machines, drones, muscle mass, artists, or gifts of God, they will be treated accordingly. Thus conceptions and kinds of work abound. Their variety reflects differing views about the goals of human life: to secure an ample pension, to provide for material needs and wants, to increase the amount of beauty in the world, to give order and purpose in a seemingly chaotic universe, to leave marks or monuments of immortality, or simply to pass the time and stave off boredom. But what is work itself?

This is a surprisingly difficult question to answer, for throughout our history strikingly different demands on our time and energy have been made. In hunter-gatherer societies people spent less time foraging for food and meeting home needs than we might think. A significant amount of time, depending on the region and time of year, could be spent on what we would call leisure, artistic, or ritual activities. It is hard to know how these people would have described "work," or if they would even understand the way we use the term today. It was only as human beings began developing agricultural societies about ten thousand years ago that economic and class structures more closely resembling our own emerged. Since the growth, storage, distribution, and protection of food called for the invention of worker, managerial, clerical, military, and religious classes, it makes more sense to speak here about fairly clearly defined spheres of "work."

This brief history shows that human activity, even as it takes on characteristics we would more readily notice as work, was integrally tied to the maintenance of one's livelihood, to the securing of the means of life: food, shelter, and protection. In the last several centuries this connection between work and livelihood has undergone a profound transformation with the introduction of wage-labor systems. In this context people take on jobs that have little to do with their livelihood. They take them to make money, which will then be used to buy the things they need to live. There is a world of difference in meaning between work done for money or a faraway boss and work done to meet personally or locally determined needs. The development of wage labor is of crucial significance because it led to the commodification of work, the buying and selling of time, skills, and energy. Now work is easily reduced to "just a job," having little connection to a larger world of value and significance. Work often carries little personal interest or communal importance because it is not an integral part of a life-promoting, life-sustaining context. Indeed, modern work, rather than being an activity that connects diverse human needs and desires, is often symptomatic of a life that is fragmented and without a unifying context. Depending on what we do, it can even be the occasion for considerable resentment.

There is a close association between work and personal identity. Through our work we give expression to what (if anything) we love and admire, respect and yearn for. This is why on a first meeting we ask people what they do. When we do not have a say over the nature and objectives of work because they are all decided by an unseen boss or unknown stockholders, or understand and respect the limiting contexts (biological and social) of our work, as increasingly happens in the context of global markets and corporate culture, it is likely that we are functioning as anonymous and easily interchangeable drones. Who wants to make a personal investment in work that does not honor workers or those for whom the work is performed? Who wants to devote themselves to a task they do not really believe in? There is an important difference between work that enriches a few at the expense of the many and work that harmonizes and strengthens workers and the communities of which they are a part.

Wage labor is the system in which most of us work today. We don't appreciate, at least not to the extent that our foremothers and forefathers did, the experience of working directly for our own livelihood or for the well-being of local, communal needs. For us, work has become highly specialized and fragmented, the movement of a tiny cog in the vast and largely unintelligible global machine. It is hard for us to think clearly about what our work is ultimately for and whether it promotes the good of others. Indeed, we may well experience a life crisis when it dawns on us that we no longer know why we go to work or have good reasons for doing the work we do.

This is where our reflection about work and its significance must begin. Why work? At this fundamental level of questioning, the connection between work and the Sabbath becomes clearer.

Why Work?

If human delight finds its model and goal in God's delighting in creation, so too human work finds its inspiration and fulfillment in God's own work of healing, restoring, strengthening, and maintaining the life of creation. Our work, if it is to be good, must line up sympathetically and harmoniously with God's. Of course, a crucial distinction between God's work and our own must be maintained. Our work is carried out at the expense of others. To secure our physical needs we must destroy and kill. God does not eat creatures to survive, nor does God create due to some internal lack, but we do. In this sense, our work can never equal God's.[1] What God requires of us is that we try to work in ways that minimize the destructive toll. And so human work, while it may not be a curse, must always live with the burden of presupposing death and dismemberment. We must acknowledge and understand this burden and not make light of it. Good work attempts, through various creative means and with the help of others, to honor and give thanks for the gifts we use and (too often wastefully) consume.

As we embark on this journey, we can be assured that God's desire to be with us in our daily work is no less intense than the desire to be with us in worship. God has chosen to identify with us in the incarnate Son and is committed to abide with us in the twists and turns of our finitude through the giving of the Spirit. Moreover, in our being and doing God aims to realize an intention greater than anything we can imagine on our own. From a Sabbath point of view, human life is not exhausted in the satisfaction of personally understood needs. The goal of all life, and thus also the purpose and manner of our work, extends beyond narrowly defined human interests to include the convivial peace of creation as a whole.

The inauguration of the Sabbath means that no work is purely mundane. Every bit of it, when seen in the appropriate light and performed in a proper spirit, can be the occasion for the glorification of God and the occasion for God's delight.

The way work and vocation have traditionally been understood, though not always with sufficient emphasis, is on the basis of humans' being created in the image of God. Though we are creatures who share in the fate of other creatures—we are born, experience suffering and joy, and will die—our existence is elevated by our unique calling and responsibility to highlight and promote the presence of God within creation and to enable creatures to share in the praise of God their Maker. As Claus Westermann has put it, *imago Dei* teaches that "the relationship to God is not something which is added to human existence; humans are created in such a way that their very existence is intended to be their relationship to God."[2] Our entire life, and thus also our work, must be understood and carried out in orientation to and conversation with God. Practically speaking, this means that whenever we embark upon some work we will ask how well it links up with or continues the work of God. Work that eviscerates whole species or that compromises the health of coworkers and communities will simply not be acceptable: it is an affront to God.

We do not exist for ourselves alone or by means of our own strength and wits. Not only do we depend upon the gifts of God for our livelihood and well-being, but the very liveliness we embody is to testify to the sustaining, healing, reconciling, celebrating intentions of God. Here we need to remember that God created the world and a purpose for it at the same time, a goal that I have summed up as *menuha*. As *imago Dei*, as God's embodied representatives on earth, humankind's central and abiding vocation is to work to our best ability, and with God's help, to make sure that creation honors God and continues to be a source of delight to God. Our most fundamental work, as well as the many permutations it can take, must grow out of this divine calling. Human work and creativity are at their most authentic best when they increase the possibilities for mutual delight.

A considerable amount of the work performed today, in terms of both the manner and the objectives of the work, does not bring honor to God or facilitate mutual delight. For many of us work is simply a chore, the thing we do to pay our ever-increasing bills. It does not often inspire us to realize our potential as servants and caretakers of creation, nor does it encourage us to promote the well-being of those we work with or for. Sometimes we feel that our work does not even matter. We do not see how what we do contributes to the healing and strengthening of our communities and homes. Many of us can't wait for the weekend to come along as an escape from work. Our craving for the weekend implies an often unspoken condemnation of the workaday week. This is deeply troubling, for it suggests worker lives that are anxious, depressed, dispirited, complacent, or even hostile. Consider in this context the words of Wendell Berry: "To work without pleasure and affection, to make a product that is not both useful and beautiful, is to dishonor God, nature, the thing that is made, and whomever it is made for. This is blasphemy: to make shoddy work of the work of God."[3]

Too seldom do we consider how our work might be either blasphemous or an occasion for God's praise. Perhaps this is because we have been trained to think that blaspheming and praising are things we do exclusively with our mouths and not with our hands and feet. But scripture will not allow this neat division between head and body. According to the prophet Isaiah, for instance, God will not hear the spoken prayers or praise of the violent and dishonest:

> When you stretch out your hands
>   I will hide my eyes from you;
> even though you make many prayers,
>   I will not listen;
>   your hands are full of blood.

Authentic worship is realized in a life of justice, and so the prophet continues:

> Wash yourselves; make yourselves clean;
>   remove the evil of your doings
>   from before my eyes;
> cease to do evil,
>   learn to do good;
> seek justice,
>   rescue the oppressed,
> defend the orphan,
>   plead for the widow.

(Isa. 1:15–17)

If in our daily work we dishonor God and creation, how can we expect that God will take seriously our Sunday efforts at worship?

A Transformed Workplace

Churches, insofar as they want to be worshiping Sabbath communities, must overcome the barriers that currently separate work life from church life. They must not succumb to the compartmentalizing mentality that (safely) allows us to sequester matters of faith in a building or in the purely private realm. Faith claims and concerns the whole person, and given that work is one of the primary means we have for developing and expressing who we are, work (as well as play, leisure, and worship) must be integrated within faith's journey. Work must be integrated because in our exercise of it we have the opportunity to develop into the persons God wants us to be.

Many of our work contexts degrade workers and their work environments—think of the many minimum-wage jobs that are without benefits, the many factories that pour poisons into waterways and the air and thus render residential neighborhoods foul, unsightly, and unsafe. Christians need to be involved in the transformation of places of work so that they will promote justice, beauty, and peace—these being the indispensable contexts for God's and our own delight. To do this we first need to be more attentive to how our work alleviates or contributes to the desecration of creation and the dismemberment of communities. When we make shoddy, cheap, or ugly products, we defile creation by using natural resources to no good end. When we artificially create needs and wants in other people, as we do through ubiquitous advertising campaigns, we take part in turning them into anxious, ungrateful, hapless, even resentful consumers.

Advocating for a just workplace does not mean arguing for a utopia. Even if Christians were to become committed to the goal of Sabbath joy, it is highly unlikely that anything like the overthrow of a wage-labor system would come about. Our goal, rather, should be to transform particular workplaces and inspire specific workers or working groups to make Sabbath peace and delight their highest priority. Practically speaking, this means that employers and employees together will strive to find ways to demonstrate care for each other, for products made and services rendered, and for the natural and social contexts upon which our work depends and to which it is eventually directed. Workers will be treated fairly and with kindness, and our natural environment will be respected and cared for. If this is to happen, employers, workers, and shareholders must come together face to face and speak with each other regularly, so that they can learn and understand what each other's needs, constraints, and aspirations are. They must come together so they can see the effects of decisions that might otherwise be made without sufficient regard for the health and safety of workers and communities.

No doubt this recommendation will sound hopelessly naive to some, given the cutthroat global marketplace. To be competitive employers must forever be attentive to the bottom line, which often means that every cost must be cut to the bone. Cost cutting may entail the sacrifice of worker benefits and safety, environmental protections and sustainability, as well as corporate responsibility to the community in the forms of appropriate taxation, local investment, and community sponsorships. The problem with this "realism" of the bottom line is that it simply accepts and does not challenge the degradation of workers, products, and environments. This is lunacy, for how can one promote a good life and a healthy creation while condoning practices that steadily erode and undermine them? Business that is informed by Sabbath teaching must practically demonstrate ways in which workers and their communities can be strengthened and protected, rather than defeated, by their work.

Consider the inspiring example of the lobster fishers of Monhegan Island off the coast of Maine. Not until the bitter cold of December 1 do they lay their lobster traps. During the milder months of July through November they do not fish, believing that lobsters need time off from our unrelenting extractive toll. Their decision, from one angle, makes excellent business sense, because their fresh winter lobster (with more meat) can obtain a premium price. And because their lobsters have not been overfished, they can reliably expect high yields.

In 1995, however, lobster fishers from the mainland began to encroach on their protected territory, clearly envious of their rich yields. The scene got ugly and violent. The Monhegan fishers turned to the law and the legislature to protect their lobsters and their livelihood. In a decision that surprised almost everyone, the state legislature decided overwhelmingly against the mainland encroachers and in favor of the Monhegan lobster fishers. The law gave these islanders control over their own fisheries and forbade outside interference.[4]

This story demonstrates the possibility and the compatibility of wise stewardship and good business. While other lobster fishers were decimating their lobster populations by overfishing—driven only by short-term financial gain—the Monhegan fishers voluntarily restricted their fishing activity to a long-term, less extractive sustainable level. In taking care of their lobsters they were at the same time taking care of their families and assuring the economic vitality of their small island. To be successful, however, they had to resist—legally in this case—the destructive pressure of their profit-seeking neighbors. The scale of their operation was small enough that the Monhegan lobster fishers could see directly the effects of their good stewardship. This enabled them to work within a Sabbath framework, even though they did not necessarily choose their course with an explicit Sabbath motive (their story does not mention a religious inspiration).

Work as Worship

A healthy work environment ought to help workers see their activity as an extension or a concrete manifestation of their worship life. Benedictine monks understood this when they adopted as one of their mottos *Laborare est orare*, "To work is to pray." The reference to prayer did not simply mean a petitioning of God for aid. In our worship and prayer we come to a fuller, more honest appreciation of the fact that we are always already surrounded by gift upon gift, though we often fail to handle them as such. A prayerful life acknowledges and celebrates the goodness of God and honors and cherishes the gifts of God—food and air, heat and light, family and friendship—by treating them with respect and care. Prayer is first and foremost the attentive activity that turns us to the world so that we can see its need and potential. It is an honest, detailed, nonevasive, patient regard for others that enables us to see them as gifts from God. Thus a prayerful life replaces the desire to bend the world to our own satisfaction with the desire to see God magnified and praised.

When God made creation, its goodness, its delightfulness, was seen in the fact that each member was free to pursue its end. Of course, this freedom is not without limits, since the flourishing of any particular creature occurs in relation to a wide and complex web of interdependencies. Each member of creation, we might say, in being itself contributes to the whole and thus realizes a potential that is conducive of further flourishing and yet more life. Because God's work is forever informed by love, it cherishes the integrity of creatures and their ability to be, while strengthening the biological and social contexts of the whole creation. If our work is animated by this godly concern, it too will promote the good of others. It will issue in a world that is more beautiful and meaningful. As the English social critic Eric Gill once put it, "Beauty is the Love of God sensible in [our] work . . . it is holiness visible."[5] With our hands we confirm the presence of God in this life by performing work that is inspired by God's own generosity and care.

Our praying orientation has a most practical effect: the affirmation and celebration of others' ability to be what God wants them to be. This is not easily done, particularly in a consumer culture premised on ignorance and ingratitude and an economy too much dependent on unnecessary destruction and waste. Because we do not see, appreciate, or understand where consumable items come from or how they came to be, we cannot really measure their costliness or sense how precious they are. This lack often renders whatever gratitude we express shallow and naive. This is why prayer must always be rooted in a life of patient attention and sustained responsibility for the many goods we live from. It is time we learn to pray seriously with our eyes wide open and with a fuller awareness of the contexts of our living. Only then will our work become salutary and a delight to God.

If we remember that our work is in some measure to be patterned on God's own work, and if we recall that God's work is throughout informed by love—indeed the whole of creation is the concrete expression of that love—then our work must express love for coworkers, for things made or services provided, and for the natural and communal contexts of work.

> Good human work honors God's work. Good work uses no thing without respect, both for what it is in itself and for its origin. It uses neither tool nor material that it does not respect and that it does not love. It honors nature as a great mystery and power, as an indispensable teacher, and as the inescapable judge of all work of human hands. It does not dissociate life and work, or pleasure and work, or love and work, or usefulness and beauty.[6]

Work must be informed by a disposition of considerate care that takes into account the needs of those we work with and for. We should always ask: How does the work we are about to do bring benefits to those around us? Does this work respect the integrity of others or in some way impede their ability to be what God wants them to be? Is our activity primarily about self-glorification?

As we begin to ask these kinds of questions regularly, we may well come to realize that much of our work is inappropriate and unnecessary: inappropriate because it does not further others' happiness and health and unnecessary because it serves only the tiny aim of self-advancement. In our time many people describe themselves as workaholics, addicted to work and voluntarily spending excessively long hours at work. (To be sure, there are many among us who work an excessive number of hours out of sheer economic desperation and injustice. These people are not workaholics because they did not voluntarily choose to work such long hours.) Workaholism leads to the neglect of family and community, the redirecting of our attention away from the happiness and well-being of those we live among. Does this trend reflect pervasive discontentment and insecurity among us, a deadening of our senses and attention, and thus a profound inability to find joy in rest and in celebration? Are we so bloated with our sense of self-importance that we can no longer trust God to provide adequately for us? We need to be much more attentive to the nature and patterns of work, because its abuse is a primary obstacle to fulfilling our highest calling, which is to celebrate the gifts of God and in so doing participate in the *menuha* of God.

For most of our history people have worked very hard for long hours, without the expectation of vacation or retirement benefits. These people could not be fairly described as workaholics. The crucial difference lies in the kind of work performed. Theirs was work performed in an integrated life context: it was done mostly at home with family for the purpose of meeting fundamental and locally determined needs. Much of our work lacks this interconnectedness and life-unifying potential. It is carried out away from our family and home, and often its purpose has little to do with daily needs or responsibilities. This sort of work makes it much more difficult for us to become alive to those around us. Here work is not about supporting or strengthening communal livelihood. It is in many instances a distraction from our home, even an escape from our household's demands and potential joys.

Given the loneliness and meaninglessness of much contemporary work, it may be time to argue for a higher estimation of physical labor performed in concert with others. Physical labor, work that exercises the body, is not held in high regard these days. We think it is beneath us, a sign that we are not well educated or well trained. This is a tragedy because it denies what is utterly basic about us: that we are bodily beings that must make our way through the world by engaging physical realities like soil, flesh, rock, water, and wood. When we disparage physical work, we close ourselves off from a sympathetic and far-reaching engagement with the stuff of God's handiwork. We also limit the likelihood that we will work together with others in necessary, life-supporting activities.

Here the example of Eric and Mary Brende is illuminating. Shortly after getting married, they decided to live for several months in a community committed to farming with as little electricity and fossil fuel as possible. They chose this community because they saw here an opportunity to live more closely with other people and with the earth—there would be fewer technological devices to broker and limit their contact with each other, they would remove themselves from careerist pressure to get ahead and make something "important" of their lives. As they began their physical labors, something they had been taught to dread as mind numbing and exhausting, they made a most surprising discovery: "Gradually, as you applied yourself to your task, the threads of friendship and conversation would grow and connect you to laborers around you. Then everything suddenly became inverted. You'd forget you were working and get caught up in the camaraderie, the sense of lightened effort. . . . Work folded into fun and disappeared. Friendship, conversation, exercise, fresh air, all melded together into a single act of mutual self-forgetting."[7]

Though this description may sound too cheerful or sunny (after all, some work, whether individually or socially performed, is taxing and miserable), it nonetheless tells us that when work is performed together, the sociality can make the work lighter and fill it with meaning. It is done together because it is of direct benefit to the parties involved. Compare the loneliness and sensed futility of so much of our own work. Physical, social labor is so important, from a Sabbath point of view, because it becomes a concrete means through which we enact and honor the connections and relationships of dependence that make our lives possible. Far from being beneath us, it lifts us all up, as we see and appreciate that we need each other and can be a help to each other.

Good work draws us closer to each other and into the world, nearer to God's grace and love, so that we can more honestly appreciate the costliness and goodness of life. As we move closer we will gradually shed the layers of anxiety and discontentment that otherwise shroud our working lives; we will see that we are everywhere supported by God's intention for abundant life. Work need not be understood as a curse. It can instead be one of our most practical means to contentment. Contentment, as Donald Hall has described it, "is work so engrossing that you do not know that you are working."[8] There is an essential paradox here: to be fully content, you cannot be conscious of your contentment. If this is true, then work is like making love. You lose yourself in the activity. It is nothing like drudgery or a chore, because we are totally absorbed in the loveliness and worthiness of what engages us, finding in that engagement our joy and our life. When work is governed by this absorbedness, Sabbath worship and praise will follow naturally and inevitably. Indeed, the praise will have already begun—and not only on Sundays.

I have been arguing that authentic work is one of the primary means we have to share in God's own continuing work of building and maintaining creation. Whatever work we perform, then, is premised on the understanding that our exertion is finally derivative, utterly dependent on God's grace as its sustaining and inspirational heart. The many indicators of work's current malfunction—workaholism, worker anxiety and stress, social fragmentation and strife, massive environmental destruction—suggest that at a very deep level we have lost faith in God's goodness. We have lost our appreciation for the loveliness of others and have turned our faithlessness into widespread abuse and exploitation. Rather than submitting to the grace of God, we have embarked upon the total management of the world. We are unable to let creation be itself, or to receive the world as a gift. We have come to think that whatever value is in this world will be the direct result of *our* doing, thus forgetting that *God's* doing goes before all of our own.

We are in desperate need of a new conception of work and a widespread discussion of what it is and what it is finally for. Sabbath people, those who understand that the goal of life is for all of us to share in the delight of God, are ideally situated to help that discussion along. As we proceed, Berry's words can help us appreciate our work as a contribution in praise of God's own work:

> And yet no leaf or grain is filled
> By work of ours; the field is tilled
> And left to grace. That we may reap,
> Great work is done while we're asleep.[9]

8

Sabbath at Home

■ Homes are in trouble. Schoolteachers regularly report that many of their students, rich and poor, come to class inappropriately dressed and fed, are poorly behaved, and show signs of neglect and abuse. Their inability to get along with classmates, as well as their frustrations and anger with learning, are often attributable to boredom, conflict, tension, disorder, or unrest at home. Many children fail to find their homes and their families to be places of nurture and support, structure and inspiration. Thus life itself is an ordeal. Not knowing where they are at home, they find it that much more difficult to understand who and where they are in the world. Not surprisingly, their modes of self and world discovery often take a violent or destructive form.

It is common, and far too easy, to blame the waywardness of our youth on violent, promiscuous, or nihilistic TV programming, movies, video games, and the Internet. This approach assumes that the causes of our trouble come from sources that are imported into the home, and thus it leaves the structure of the home itself unquestioned. We need to ask more fundamental questions: Why has screen entertainment become such an attractive, even necessary, option for so many families? (As an experiment, try unplugging the television and home computer for a month and see what happens.) Does this necessity spring from family members' basic unavailability to each other or from a failure to find in our interpersonal relations a deep fund of joy, inspiration, and contentment?

Households have been under assault since long before the intervention of entertainment media. In many instances this assault was carried out under the banner of economic necessity. Land consolidation, the advent of factory work, and the growth of expanding, even international markets have meant that work has increasingly had to be done away from the home and with a purpose less directly connected with the needs of the household, family members, and the local community. The fragmentation of the day into work life and home life, as well as the growing separation between individual purpose and family goals, professional work and community service, has meant that homes now function under severe pressures from within and from without. How shall we reunite the many strands of community, family, and home life that are currently moving in different directions?

Our culture's mythology states that in "the good old days" families were much more cohesive units and homes were places of nurture and refuge. Dads went to work while moms stayed home to make sure that everything ran smoothly and efficiently. Meals were cooked, clothes were washed and ironed, the house was spic and span, and the homework was always done. But as moms "went to work" too (as if they didn't "work" before!), the balance of home life went awry, and children became the most visible casualties. With both parents working, there is hardly enough time or energy left over to get even the basics of home life done. Practical necessity dictates that we outsource (and pay handsomely for) many of the tasks that used to be performed by family members in the home, like the care of infants, young children, and our elderly; food preparation; house, garden, and lawn care; athletic, musical, or artistic development; counseling; fun and recreation; and religious education. Not surprisingly, many people think the best solution is to compel women back into the house so that balance, order, and nurture can be restored.

This is not a solution, not only because it trades on questionable assumptions about gender roles and the true nature of work but also, and more important, because it fails to understand what the purpose of a home is. It assumes that the idealized Beaver Cleaver–type home, consisting of two parents, two kids, the dog and cat, and now the vacation boat and house on the side, is what a home should be. We continue to be fed highly stylized portrayals of home in the very lucrative "home improvement" industry, where, if you have enough money, you can have the look of practically any home you want. But through most of human history, and for the great majority of people, homes included the extended family, all of whom were focused on the care of land and animals. Further, homes opened out into local communities and habitats so that their needs and potential could be sensed and engaged. These facts make it easy to see how flimsy and recent the "bring Mom home" assumption really is. From an agrarian point of view, one could even describe the 1950s "golden age" home as a perversion of what home and family life should be.

What Is a Home?

In centuries past, work was done at the home—one did not leave to "go to work" or go to school—and in a cooperative manner: the work of the husband, wife, children, and extended family members was complementary because it shared a common purpose and need. In fact, the work was a cohesive glue for the household. Contrast with today's household: each day each member leaves for a destination that may be unfamiliar to the others—office, factory, classroom, fitness center or spa—and individual motivation and purpose are mostly disconnected from the motivations and purposes of the family. In many instances we do not know or appreciate what each other is doing. And so in our time, homes are as often places of division and ignorance (how many kids really understand what their parents do for a living?) as they are places of common cause, vision, and effort. We have been taught to value individual fulfillment rather than kinship and communal solidarity.

The way homes function and how we think about them (especially through the more recent lenses of television and advertising) has changed considerably over time. Not all of these changes have contributed to stronger or better homes, homes that make something like a Sabbath experience possible. But the households of past centuries had their troubles too. We should be trying to imagine and then implement homes wherein peace, joy, and delight, what I have been calling the *menuha* of God, can find their most visible manifestation. If we can do this, we may yet learn to see our households as "a little church" or "Christ's general receptacle" (St. John Chrysostom) in which our life together participates in the triune life of God.[1]

A home cannot be reduced to the physical structure we call a house. Plenty of people have lived in houses yet testify to a sense of homelessness. For a house to be a home, it must be more than a physical space and become a spiritual center. In the process, the physical space cannot be disregarded but must be incorporated into a spiritual calling. Mere space becomes a place where people find their identity and vocation, their meaning and purpose, their joy and delight. Home is not simply a refuge or a place where we hide from the world, but is rather the site where we are taught and empowered to more fully and justly engage family members, neighbors, communities, strangers, natural habitats, and the broader culture. What makes a house a home is the complex set of relations that are discovered, forged, and celebrated through time among family, friends, guests, animals, plants, even water, soil, and sunlight. In order for a house to become a home, then, creative forms of spiritual as well as physical building must take place. Only then does it really become a shelter.

For our house to be a shelter, more than our protection from the weather is at stake. In the visionary words of Gaston Bachelard, "The house shelters day-dreaming, the house protects the dreamer, the house allows one to dream in peace."[2] As children grow, daydreaming is vital to their development. They need safe, intimately known places in which the important work of value clarification and integration can occur. Houses—places of intimacy and familiarity—are important because they are the concrete spaces through which people develop deep relationships and responsibilities and learn to understand themselves and what matters in life. We need places of intimacy so that we can experience the nearness and closeness of others—see where and how we fit in. It is through such belonging that young people often come to the realization of what they want and need to do in life. This is why we often have such fond memories of the house we grew up in and find it a great sadness when the house is destroyed or dramatically altered. The house, says Bachelard, is our first "world," the place wherein we become alive and alert to others. "Life begins well, it begins enclosed, protected, all warm in the bosom of the house."[3] The home is fundamental to human existence because it is here that we learn the art and the discipline of fidelity to each other, without which we can scarcely imagine the maintenance, let alone joy, of social and biological life together.

This elevation of home as a place of intimacy and a school for fidelity that forms and inspires us to engage the wide world may seem, at first glance, to contradict Jesus's words: "Foxes have holes, and birds of the air have nests; but the Son of Man has nowhere to lay his head" (Matt. 8:20; Luke 9:58). Jesus said he did not have a house, a permanent mailing address, presumably because he was always on the move. Moreover, his attitude about home and family may appear hostile to the kind of intimacy that is constitutive of a home. Consider his words to the group that was sent by his family asking for him: "'Who are my mother and my brothers?' And looking at those who sat around him, he said, 'Here are my mother and my brothers! Whoever does the will of God is my brother and sister and mother'" (Mark 3:33–35; cf. Matt. 12:46–50; Luke 8:19–21). This rebuke clearly challenges contemporary notions of the home as a private place of retreat and escape from the world and its problems. But does it also call into question the intimacy and inspiration, the integration and clarification of values and vision, that are the basis of a genuine home?

There are good reasons to think not. What Jesus is doing in statements like this is helping us see that certain kinds of intimacy are unhealthy: they deflect us from the loyalty and familiarity that mark a truly faithful life.

Indeed, kinds of familiality exist that actually get in the way of God's building of the kingdom, and so we should not be surprised to hear Jesus say that brothers will betray each other, children will rise up against their parents, and forms of hatred will arise leading to death, all because of one's loyalty to God (Mark 13:12–13). Jesus's unsentimental words about family will be scandalous only to those who refuse intimacy with and fidelity to God as the foundation upon which other forms of familiarity can be built.

Though homes are enclosures of a sort, they must not close us off from the call of God or shield us from the needs of neighbors and strangers. When we embark on a path of friendship with God, when we fully enter into God's family as devoted children, we enter into new ways of relating to each other and to the places in which we live. Jesus says in Luke 14:26 that if we want to enter into God's family (by becoming his disciples) we must first "hate" our biological father and mother, wife and children, brothers and sisters. A family is not something we have by the natural accident of birth but something we commit and pledge our allegiance to. Home is not destroyed by Jesus's call to discipleship. It is radically reconstituted so that our identities and vocations, our presence in God's world with a godly purpose and direction, can take shape in families that have God as their Father and forgiveness, reconciliation, service, and hospitality as their animating center.

In these "hard sayings" Jesus is showing us how the circles of fidelity we choose for ourselves are far too narrow; these circles need to be expanded to include the whole creation. To be at home in a Christian sense is to be in God's family and creation and to find our hearts animated by the intentions of God. It is to be in solidarity with the whole creation, so that our collective joy and delight might be more complete. When as a people we are inspired by God to do the communal work of building God's kingdom—a kingdom marked by restored and convivial relationships, good food and drink, the recovery of what was lost, ample generosity and celebration—we become the house of God.

Sabbath teaching, particularly the Sabbath goals of thanksgiving and praise, can play a powerful role in helping us understand and correct the distortions and malfunctions of home that are in evidence today. It keeps our focus on God's ultimate goal for all of creation. Moreover, converting our households into Sabbath homes is indispensable if we want to be Sabbath people, for without daily nurture it is highly unlikely that we will sustain the vision and the hope we enjoy in formal worship. Our daily walk must be on paths and in rooms of praise and thanksgiving: this is where we prepare our hearts for the Sabbath feast. We need our Sabbath sensibilities to be trained and refined throughout the week and in our homes so that our worship, whenever it occurs, will be genuine and true. How shall we proceed?

Building a Sabbath Home

Given that homes are first and foremost places for training in fidelity, places in which the range of our relationships and responsibilities can become clear, we need to be mindful of the practical conditions necessary for the faithful and celebratory embrace of each other. Would people, simply by looking, see that Christian homes are markedly different in their architectural design, the running of practical affairs, and in the ways they join up with the broader community? Are our homes places wherein we take time to be attentive and responsive to family members, neighbors, local habitats, and communities? Are we intentional about cultivating the skills that equip us to recognize and address need? Most of us would readily admit that in these areas we are seriously deficient. In fact, the notion that we might have the time, patience, and attention to fully be available to each other will strike many as an impossible dream. Our cultural context does not allow it.

One serious impediment is recent residential architectural design. The very physical shape and arrangement of our homes communicate anonymity, separation, and movement away from each other. The garage is given copious pride of place, large and in front, demonstrating that cars and the mobility they afford are high priorities. Noticeably absent from our design is a welcoming front porch, a place that looks out into the wider community and that encourages time spent relaxing and conversing with each other. Backyards are small and are surrounded by privacy fences. We don't spend much time out and about; we prefer the solitude and protection of interior rooms and the control and comfort of home entertainment centers. Kitchens and dining rooms, which used to be focal points of gathering, places where people could interact face to face (rather than around a television or computer screen), have been significantly reduced in size and use because we can presume that people spend time or eat less and less together. And so our architecture, even the way we arrange our furniture, rather than fostering and communicating our life together, in fact encourages separation from each other.

Besides space, we should think about how time is currently experienced in the home. For many of us, time is precisely what we do not have. From the moment we get up in the morning until we go to bed at night, we race from place to place and from one obligation to the next. If you are part of a family with children, there are endless kid activities—school rehearsals and functions, art or music lessons, athletic practices and events, not to mention social activities—that keep you constantly on the go. The family vehicles (we can't do it all with just one) resemble taxicabs that carry clients from home to school to practice to lesson to fast-food joint to friend's house to youth function to grocery store to the mall, and then back home again. Even if there are no kids at home, there is no end to work responsibilities, committee assignments, volunteer tasks. By the time we finally settle down for the night we are exhausted, having been barely able to get the laundry and basic house maintenance done. To suggest that we should, in the face of all this flurry and fury, create quality time to be fully present to each other seems to be asking for the impossible.

When we submit to this sort of schedule we are consenting to cultural patterns long in the making, patterns that have become so ingrained that we accept them as normal and thus beyond question or critique. But is it normal to think that our pace of life should be one that leads to exhaustion, hypertension, anxiety, boredom, and despair? No doubt the boosters of the current global economic order think it essential that we stay on the fast-flying, risk-taking consumer and job treadmill, because in doing so we vastly enrich the investors who fuel the globalization bandwagon. But surely this is ridiculous. Our frantic pace is unprecedented in history. So-called primitives, ranging from hunter-gatherers to peasants, would be astounded at the lists of things we think we "have" to do. Whereas ancient and premodern societies assumed ample time for personal and communal rest and genuine festivity, we scramble for release and then feel guilty that we have not done enough.

The first step toward becoming a Sabbath home will therefore require that we learn to say no to the many pressures to do or accomplish more. We need to keep firmly in mind what all this striving is ultimately for. We need to ask, how does this activity or that purchase contribute to or take away from our capacity to be present and available to each other and to honor and celebrate the gifts of God among us? Here we must develop our attentive powers in new ways, because we are easily fooled about what constitutes a help or hindrance. Our homes are filled with labor and time-saving devices, ranging from microwaves and dishwashers to automatic sprinklers and bread machines. Given the ubiquity of these many gadgets, one would think that we would have ample time to spare. But in fact we do not. Why? The answer is not just that we fill up our time with other tasks but also that we actively devote much of our energy to the procurement of ever more "necessities." We work harder and longer to buy more stuff that, in the end, we need to worry and fuss about because it does not work properly, breaks, or is quickly made obsolete by the new and improved version of the same thing.

Think too about taken-for-granted necessities like automobiles and televisions, which in pervasive and sometimes subtle ways militate against the possibility of time together. Is it a good idea to have a TV in every room when we know that it will siphon attention and focus away from each other, or to encourage activities that require extensive car use since these will restrict group participation? Even the place where we choose to live can make a powerful difference. For instance, if we purchase a home in the suburbs or exurbs, what Jane Jacobs calls "blights of dullness," it is much more likely that we will be utterly dependent on automobiles to get us everywhere we need to go. As new urban theorists like Jacobs and Eric Jacobsen can tell us, in postmodern suburbia the mundane, utterly practical, concrete contexts in which people can casually bump into each other and strike up a conversation have all but disappeared. Without sidewalks, boulevards, local parks, town centers, and the like, the occasions and places for people to meet and greet and develop an understanding of issues of common concern have vanished. We all become trapped in our houses, isolated from without and within, and, through our walls and fences, made oblivious to the many layers of relationship and interdependence that literally and figuratively nurture us. Moreover, the physical arrangement of our living places, with their emphasis on independence and privacy, and the practical modes of our movement, which emphasize personal freedom and independence, all contribute to character traits that are squarely against biblical goals of mutual forbearance, upbuilding, and celebration.[4]

A Place for a Sabbath Feast

For Sabbath people, it will not be enough simply to resist cultural forms and expectations. We also need to develop positive practices that will draw us closer to each other. Albert Borgmann has wisely suggested that homes and communities recover what he calls "focal practices":[5] the set of personal and communal habits that bring people into regular and sympathetic face-to-face contact. In our time of hyperreality, when relationships are increasingly mediated by technological gadgets and automobiles, and when speed overwhelms our capacity for attention and patience, a focal practice compels us to take stock of how we live from and through each other. These are practices like neighborhood Little League and a community orchestra, activities that bring us into closer contact with each other so that we can directly see how we need and benefit each other and thus really ought to make more time to celebrate and enjoy what we live together.

Consider something basic like a family meal. This is a practice that is quickly disappearing, if it has not vanished already. The reason has to do with our fast and fragmenting schedules. Home life has become geared to individual quests, which means that adults play the role of managers. Those responsible for food are reduced to making sure the fuel is available as needed. Because our needs and schedules are so varied, we cannot eat at the same time. We eat on the go, using the drive-through at the fast-food place or the multiple prepackaged convenience foods available at superstores—all we need to do is pop them in the microwave and be off. Or we eat alone, at a counter or on a tray, catching up on rest or the latest TV programming.

If as Sabbath people we were to insist on regular family meals and turn our eating into a focal practice, this would constitute a revolutionary witness to the world. What would be involved? First, eating would become more genuinely cooperative, as household members would have to reach some agreement about what to eat. This in turn would presuppose an understanding of what people enjoy eating and an appreciation for good food. This latter appreciation, in turn, would presuppose an understanding of our current food economy and its many abuses. Can we really enjoy a wholesome meal if the food is produced in an unwholesome manner, or in a way that exhausts or poisons land and water or unjustly treats farmers and food producers? Eating healthy food will most likely require us to shop differently by frequenting local markets and participating in direct marketing with farmers, or to become gardeners and grow some food for ourselves. This small, practical shift, when done by enough people, will have enormous implications for our food economy—the big, heavily subsidized producers will be replaced by local organic growers. It will also mean large changes in the structure our days—gardening, with its slower and more patient rhythms, will now take a good bit of our days. The net effect will be that we will think differently about food. It will be understood no longer as mere fuel but as the gift of God that it is. By becoming more intentional about what we eat and more involved in the food economy, we will become better stewards and servants of God's creation and more attuned to the grace of God among us.

The importance of a family garden should not be underestimated. What is at issue is not simply the production of a few vegetables or the pleasures of beautiful flowers but the equally important, palpable sense that we live *through* and *by* the gifts of others. As every good gardener knows, the processes of life and death are beyond our control (though we can be purely destructive in our control and our overuse of poisons). We put our seed in the ground, tend it with the best care we can, and then must trust in and rely on the beneficence of God to take over. This process is a practical lesson in humility and an apprenticeship in appropriate creaturehood, the sense that we live by a grace that comprehends us even as we do not comprehend it. Gardening teaches us to slow down (plants mature on their schedules rather than our own), be patient, cooperate, mark our interdependence, learn to share, and see the goodness of God.

But this is only the beginning. Regular family meals require that we come together. Provided that the television or stereo is not playing in the background and that telephone or beeper interruptions are ignored, the preparation and the eating of the meal, as well as its cleanup, can be occasions for sustained conversation and listening. We can be focused on each other's struggles, worries, accomplishments, and hopes. We can also learn about the larger contexts in which family members move and thus address our citizenry's narrowness and massive ignorance about local, cultural, and world affairs. In situations like this, labor-saving devices actually become impediments to our time together. For instance, the cutting of vegetables and the baking of cakes, or the washing and drying of dishes, while perhaps more easily handled by a machine, can be occasions where we enjoy good conversation and the satisfaction of having accomplished a worthwhile and household sustaining activity together. This latter benefit is not insignificant, particularly when we remember the general aimlessness that hangs as a cloud over many of our youth. People need to know they are contributing to something that matters and is life affirming. The key to making practices of this sort a success, however, is that they be properly valued and honored. Nobody wants to prepare a meal or clean up in a context of drudgery and isolation or with the sense that what they are doing does not really matter or is not affirmed and celebrated.

If we are to attend to the details of a family meal and make this a household priority, we are also going to have to reevaluate the way we think about the domestic arts. This is no small matter, for in our time we generally live with the assumption that household work is menial and beneath anyone's care. Given this assumption, we should not be shocked that our homes are in massive disarray. Nobody really aspires to house-work, nor do we compensate or celebrate those who perform it. This is a troubling state of affairs because it denies the divinely ordained human vocation: that we "serve and keep" (Gen. 2:15) the garden home God has given us. This is our fundamental and inescapable task. When we forfeit it, we seriously jeopardize the health of the garden as well as the health of our homes and families.

What are domestic arts for? At root they are about creating and sustaining the practical conditions necessary for a wholesome life together. They are about making sure that the biological, social, and family relationships that bind us to each other are properly acknowledged and nurtured. The goal is not simply utility, as when we make sure that we each have the bare necessities—clean socks and underwear, the newspaper, a bottle of water—to get by, but the creation of a pleasing and beautiful home, a place where we can come together for rest, refreshment, celebration, and further work. As we make our home and our work there beautiful, we not only make home an inviting place to be (could it be that the homelessness so many modern people feel stems from the ugliness and thoughtlessness of our homes?) but participate in the beauty that God is. St. Thomas Aquinas said this profoundly: "Beauty is a participation in the first cause, which makes all things beautiful. So that the beauty of creatures is simply a likeness of the divine beauty in which things participate."[6] Household work like home design and architecture, cleaning and repair, food preparation, the rearing of children, the counseling of friends and family, gardening and yard care all are opportunities to share in the beauty of God already at work in the world. In promoting beautiful homes (not simply stylish houses) and in committing ourselves to help habitats and people become beautiful, we amplify God's delight and our own.

Karsten Harries, a philosopher of architecture, has said that dwelling is never merely about architecture but more fundamentally about ethics. In fact architecture is our response to an essential incompleteness within our selves and expresses our need for others and for community. Homes are thus very much like gardens in that they rely on gifts (rain and sunshine) from outside: natural talent and skill, the wise counsel of neighbors and tradition, biological and geophysical sources like water and good soil, and the collective efforts and energy of friends and family members. When we make our dwellings into Sabbath homes, what we are doing is making sure that the places we live are places wherein praise and thanksgiving to God, which are the acknowledgment and celebration of these gifts, become the natural, even inevitable, outgrowth.

The praise and thanksgiving that are nurtured in the home must have hospitality as their corollary practice. To be faithful to the gifts that we are to each other means that we must turn our lives and our home into a gift that can then be given away. When God created us, God made room within the divine life for something other than Godself to be—the early church father John of Damascus described creation as God's "making room" for us to be and thrive. Remembering this, we can see that the work of creation is at root a form of hospitality. Insofar as our work is patterned on God's and shares in the divine intention that we all participate in the *menuha* of God, it must of necessity continue this work of hospitality. Just as the Garden of Eden was a hospitable feast, so too our tables and bedrooms must be open to the needs of family, neighbors, community members, and strangers. We must resist the modern tendency to close off our home from outsiders.

The principles behind biblical hospitality are not difficult to identify. The experience of Israel was marked by vulnerability, dependence, and thus reliance upon the gifts of God. The Sabbath code therefore made it clear that the Israelite nation, when somewhat established, must make every effort to take in and provide for the vulnerable and dependent in their midst. In the early church, it is significant that the Eucharist, a shared meal, was most indicative of the dawning kingdom of God and that the apostles repeatedly reminded their followers to welcome one another.

The point is not to invite only friends or people who could benefit us in some way. For hospitality to be genuinely Christian, those welcomed must be the ones who are the least, who are poor, despised, exhausted, or otherwise rejected by others. For in attending to these people we may be attending to Christ himself.

Christine Pohl has written lucidly about hospitality in the Christian tradition, its history and complex dimensions. She reminds us that hospitality is important because "to be without a place means to be detached from basic, life-supporting institutions—family, work, polity, religious community, and to be without networks of relations that sustain and support human beings."[7] We cannot be a Sabbath people when we know that many others are deprived of the sources of life that bring us joy or are denied the web of relationships that fill life with meaning and delight. No doubt it is risky, even dangerous, at times for us to open our homes to the unknown. This makes it all the more important for us to overcome the isolation that has grown between and within homes, so that hospitality can become a communal, truly ecclesial practice.

A Sabbath home is a place where people can learn the art of being faithful to each other before God. It is a place where we can accentuate and nurture the gifts of God given to us and strengthen the memberships that make us whole. It is the place where we can learn to participate in the hospitality of God by ourselves becoming hospitable to those around us in need. As we practice Sabbath keeping in our homes, we will invite God's delight to shine among us. We will also enjoy a small taste of God's heavenly feast.

9

Sabbath Economics

■ Everywhere, it seems, people are talking and are deeply concerned about economic issues and the state of the economy—except in the church. We daily monitor the stock market, pay close attention to the pronouncements of the Federal Reserve Board chairman, and panic at the latest dire prediction of this or that economist. Political leaders, corporations, and whole institutions rise and fall based on whether they benefit from or can produce economic success. As we all know, a serious economic downturn can have disastrous effects for families and local communities, as well as states and national governments.

It is right and good that we think about the economy and economic matters, for in the very practical sphere of building, purchasing and selling, trading and growing, we get to the heart of what our living is about and what most deeply inspires and sustains us. Of course, there are any number of ways that our economic thinking and acting can go astray—as when our focus is on personal gain at the expense of others, or when we practice accounting methods that conceal or do not adequately value all the costs of our living—but the point remains that if we care about life we at the same time have to be carefully attentive to the practical conditions and environments in which this living occurs. We need to make wise decisions that will best promote life's continuation and health.

Given the centrality of economic decision making for personal and social well-being, it is a curious and somewhat disconcerting fact that ministers and church people spend very little sustained time considering economic issues within the church itself and in terms of their faith commitments. There is a serious disconnect between what people profess about spiritual matters and the priorities they follow in their economic lives. The same people who insist that we take the scriptures literally on matters pertaining to the creation of the universe do not feel it necessary, in spite of explicit instructions, to sell their possessions and give the money to the poor (cf. Matt. 19:21; Mark 10:21; Luke 18:22; Acts 2:45). Whether we care to admit it or not, the church bears a great responsibility for the fact that we are abettors and willing participants in one of the most rapacious, violent, and destructive economies the world has ever known, an economy in which natural habitats, families and local communities, and moral principles are regularly sacrificed for the sake of financial gain.

The scriptures are clear that we simply must do better than this, and they give us several resources with which to begin our improvement. Among these, Sabbath teaching is theoretically powerful and rich but also immensely practical. As the history of Israel and the early church demonstrates, however, following this teaching is anything but easy. Though the young Hebrew nation was to set up an economy that would be in marked contrast to the violence of the Egyptian systems from which its people fled, in reality they easily succumbed to the temptations of greedy success and the injustices such success presupposes. We need to be constantly vigilant and honest with ourselves and each other about what is motivating our activity. We need prophets and the support and encouragement of communities who can help us live responsibly, fairly, and with appropriate desire. The integrity and legitimacy of the Hebrew nation, as the prophets repeatedly emphasized, depended on whether it promoted a God-inspired economy in which the hungry were fed, the poor and the orphaned well cared for, and the oppressed set free. Today we no less than they need practical, God-inspired directives for how to build communities and habitats that will be a source of mutual flourishing and a delight to God.

Starting with Principles

If we want to be a Sabbath people, we need to be intensely—daily, even hourly—aware of the priorities and principles that govern our economic activity. We can start with a fundamental and very practical question: how do we spend our money, and what do our spending patterns say about our trust in God and care for each other? This question must be raised over and over again, because the acquiring and spending of money, especially in a consumer society like ours, is the nodal point around which we structure the hours of our days. How much we spend and what we spend our money on reflect our priorities and our faith more honestly and clearly than anything we might say. Do our personal spending ledgers mirror God's own concern that families and communities, indeed the whole of creation, be thriving and well? By focusing on economic activity we gain a more intimate look at whether or not our faith has really taken hold and if it is making a difference.

When we look at the emergence of the Israelite nation, it is clear that theirs was not a capitalist, consumer society where having and spending money were the primary preoccupations. Their context was subsistence agriculture, so for them the fundamental economic question was how land and households—the twin prisms through which Israelite economic life were defined—were to be apportioned and managed. Did they treat their land and their servants or slaves in ways that reflected trust in God and a commitment to care for each other? By considering this question we can learn the principles that distinguish a Sabbath economy, principles that we can then translate into a more contemporary idiom.

For the Israelites, household activity and land management were defined in religious terms. Economic life could not be bracketed from the concerns of God, because if Israel was to be "a light to the nations" it would have to model in its practices God's intentions for creation. Among these intentions, one of the most basic is that everyone—and not simply the powerful or fortunate few—should have access to the sources of life's sustenance. Christopher Wright summarizes this point well: "The right of all people to have access to, and use of, the resources of the earth is a prior right to the right of any person or group to claim private ownership and use of some section of those resources."[1] Though families did own land, the ownership itself was always qualified by God's giving of the land as a gift. God is the ultimate owner of all land, and whatever ownership we enjoy must respect God's concern that all creation be well cared for.

God's ownership of the land was not simply a theoretical idea or pious sentiment. It had economic implications. Sabbath legislation, as reflected in Leviticus 25:23, put it this way: "The land shall not be sold in perpetuity, for the land is mine; with me you are but aliens and tenants." This prohibition against the permanent sale of land spoke to the immediate concern that a family might be forever dispossessed from their land because of some temporary hardship. As urbanites we may not think this an important matter. But in an ancient agrarian context in which virtually all the necessities of life were drawn from the soil, to be without land or without some access to it was truly disastrous. Landlessness was the gateway to destitution. This is why Israelite land management encouraged the preservation of families or households on their land and discouraged the consolidation of landholdings in the hands of a wealthy few. At stake was not simply concerns about the greedy accumulation of personal wealth but also God's promise to make sure that everyone's need was provided for. If segments of the population were denied access to the land and the material goods it provides, then God's sovereignty, faithfulness, generosity, and care would be open to question. The land is not ours to do with as we please. It is a gift given to us by God so that in our working with it the needs of all can be met. Whatever dominion over creation (Gen. 1:26–29) we enjoy, it must be seen through this practical economic lens.

It is important for us to appreciate how this economic policy developed within a Sabbath context. For instance, the policy just mentioned—that people not be permanently landless—found its clearest expression in the year of Jubilee, the Sabbath of Sabbaths. God commanded that on the fiftieth year "you shall return, every one of you, to your property and every one of you to your family" (Lev. 25:10). Those who had to sell land or household members (slaves or servants) because of dire economic circumstances should not remain in a destitute or vulnerable position forever. On the fiftieth year those who had lost their land or had been sold to another household were to be returned to their ancestral lands and families so that they could have a fresh start at living a decent life. The Jubilee proclaims liberty and release (*shemittah*) because it directly reflects God's generosity with us and God's desire that we live well on the land. As the owner of all, God could simply keep it for himself. But God does not do this. God opens his hand so that others can enjoy what God has to give. In a similar manner we are not to be tightfisted in our economic dealings, trying to secure as much for ourselves as possible. Rather, we should extend hands of mercy and compassion to those who have suffered hardship. The most direct way we can do this is to release people from their debt or bondage—think here of how personal and credit card debt keeps people chained to debilitating situations—and restore them to a position where they can have fair and equal access to the resources necessary for life.

This is a difficult principle that runs counter to many of our prevailing notions of landownership and fairness. We might even respond that it is fraught with far too many practical problems to be feasible. Do we need to rewrite bankruptcy laws or absolve developing nations of their foreign debt? What we need to remember, however, is that this Jubilee teaching, whether fully realized in history or not, held before the Israelites some very important guidelines for economic life. Among these Wright has identified four that deserve special attention. First, the sources of life must be available to be enjoyed by all. This does not mean that everyone should have the same amount of land but that all should have enough to maintain a viable household. This is the most basic or fundamental of economic principles; it flows directly from the belief that God owns everything and gives it to us as a generous gift. God's care is not limited to a select few but extends to all. Second, God's desire that all have fair access to the land means that as a society we must resist the tendency for land and wealth to accumulate in the hands of the few. For us to be successful in this regard, clear, practical measures, like the law of *shemittah,* must be in place to redress inequities and wealth polarities that would otherwise grow. Third, economic policy must be developed that promotes the vitality and flourishing of household units, since this is the place in which individual and social life are most directly nourished and sustained. Economic life must not first and foremost serve an abstract purpose like a monarchy or national interest, corporate profits, the stock market, or gross domestic product, since the promotion of such interests would readily entail the sacrificing or degradation of family units and local economies. Indeed, the protection of family and local interests stands behind Samuel's warning (in 1 Sam. 8:11–17) to the fledgling Israelite nation that the desire for a king would lead to a military draft, forced (state) labor, and taxation—burdens that would drain away resources much needed at home. And fourth, economic policy must include safety valves so that temporary economic collapse or catastrophe does not unduly limit or condemn future generations of a household. Though society will have its poor, if we claim to be people of God we must make sure that they do not become utterly ruined. It is precisely this concern that lies behind the Sabbath year provision (in Exod. 23:9–12) in which land on the seventh year is not to be harvested by the owner but released and let alone so that the poor can harvest and eat.

These four principles sprang from the Israelite experience of being a people rescued and redeemed by God. These principles could not be sustained by heroic acts of generosity or goodwill. If they were to become real at all, they had to follow from the regular remembrance of God's generosity and kindness in creating the world, forming them as a people, and leading them into the Promised Land. Sabbath year and Jubilee ordinances, as Richard Lowery observes, were the best "manifestations of God's sovereignty in Israel and the world," confirming that the Israelite people do not live by the might of their own hands but by the grace of God. "As royal householder of the nation, Yahweh's honor was at stake in the welfare of the people, particularly the most vulnerable. Social justice in Israel had a theocratic rationale. Fairness, equity, and especially care for the suffering poor were signs of Yahweh's sovereign authority among the people. Injustice and lack of compassion were acts of rebellion, public affronts to God's sovereign power."[2] Thus the economic policies encouraged by Sabbath and Jubilee teaching are not so much about the redistribution of wealth as they are about the restoration of all life to something approaching God's original and sovereign intention. This is what redemption means: to loosen the grip of injustice and oppression so that the people of God can be freed to live out the peace, joy, and delight that marked the first Sabbath sunrise. As the psalmist says, God is not only the One who made heaven and earth but also the One

> who executes justice for the oppressed;
>   who gives food to the hungry.
> The Lord sets the prisoners free;
>   the Lord opens the eyes of the blind.
> The Lord lifts up those who are bowed down;
>   the Lord loves the righteous.
> The Lord watches over the strangers;
>   he upholds the orphan and the widow,
>   but the way of the wicked he brings to ruin.
>
> (Ps. 146:7–9)

Translating Principles into Action

Given this biblical background, how do we now translate these principles into a contemporary and mostly urban idiom? How can we devise contemporary economic practices that will reflect our trust in God's great generosity and promote kindness and justice within our communities? As for the Israelites, our starting point must be the affirmation that *God's ownership of all creation comes first.* This is a basic principle with a practical significance that is often and easily missed. Consider, for instance, our attempt to get at this concept with the idea of stewardship. Though this term has been appropriated by environmentalists advocating stewardship of the earth, for most laypeople it appears on "stewardship Sunday" when the minister makes a special appeal for members to tithe in their offerings. The tithe is usually understood to be 10 percent of our earned income, though few members actually approach this percentage (if they did, churches would be flush with money).

Clearly it is important for believers to give generously and sacrificially of their income, since this simple act acknowledges that what we earn is not really ours as a permanent possession. Our giving really amounts to a giving back of gifts lavishly bestowed by God and already received by us. And so it is misleading to think that when we put some money into an offering plate we have dispensed with our economic duty or adequately acknowledged God's ownership. The problem with the tithing approach is its narrowness of vision and its assumption that the other 90 percent is somehow ours to do with as we want. The more encompassing question to ask is how our economic practices as a whole need to be changed when the totality of the economy is understood to be God's. In other words, we need to think more about God's ownership of the 90 percent than we normally do.

When we begin to think this comprehensively, we see plainly that our current industrial economy radically denies God's ownership. A comprehensive economic vision would take into account the whole creation as God's household or *oikos* (from which the word *economy* derives), for we have to assume that literally nothing escapes God's notice or care. It will not do to isolate parts of creation and deem them "useful" or "valuable" according to a self-serving human accounting framework, for the moment we do that we immediately relegate other parts to the status of useless or valueless. But that is precisely what our current economy does: it assumes that certain groups of people (mostly the rich and other people of influence) and particular sorts of resources (trees, coal, and oil) are really valuable, while other groups of people (farmers, migrant workers, service job employees) and resources (water, soil, and air—the dumping grounds for our poisons and wastes) are not. The latter group is readily sacrificed to serve the interests of the former. At other times, however, economic theory ignores altogether the gifts of creation and assumes that economic development is a feature of capital investment, applied labor, and human ingenuity alone. As Herman Daly once put it, economists are great at giving us wonderful recipes but then fail to include the ingredients list, as if we could enjoy wonderful bread without the gifts of wheat, sunshine, soil, and water. Or do we think of the economy as an animal that has a circulatory system but no digestive tract?[3] Our dependence on God for the basic sources of life is thus denied, and God's good gifts are taken for granted.

Another way to think about this is to say that our modern economy pits individual members against each other. This leads to class tension and unrest, as the gap between rich and poor steadily grows, and widespread environmental exhaustion and destruction. Such competitiveness has war as its inevitable result. This was the sort of economy that reigned in Egypt, one that could only be maintained by the whip and the threat of death against a large class of people (slaves and servants) deemed valueless and thus dispensable. As the Sabbath code makes clear, whatever rest and delight we enjoy must not be premised on the exhaustion or destruction of others. This is why Sabbath rest applied as much to aliens, servants, slaves, and even domestic animals and fields as it did to the Israelites themselves. In this Sabbath economy, if it was to be genuine, there could be no artificial or pragmatic separation of members into groups so that the one can be abused to the profit of the other.

No doubt what motivated this command was the realization that in God's economy the members of creation form an indispensable whole in which we all need each other, even if the need is not immediately apparent to us. As Wendell Berry puts it, in an economy attentive to God's encompassing ownership and care, there are no sides, not even a summing up of parts, but rather "a *membership* of parts inextricably joined to each other, receiving significance and worth from each other and from the whole."[4] In this great membership of creation we call God's economy, literally everything counts, because each part is joined to each other and the whole. The suffering of the one, given enough time, will inevitably lead to the suffering of others and of the whole. In this suffering, communities come to eventual ruin, and the *menuha* of God is denied.

When we recognize that God's ownership comes first and that the whole of creation represents God's household, it is clear that in our economies we must make every effort to fit harmoniously within the limits and possibilities God's generosity allows. This is very difficult given the individualism that permeates our culture and the many ways in which we insulate ourselves from the effects of our decisions and actions. We do not, for the most part, think and decide with a natural, social, or civic body firmly in view. As numerous political philosophers have pointed out, it would be difficult to envision and implement a forum in which genuine conversation about a "common good" could occur (let alone decide upon that good). But this is exactly what we must do—and what local churches are uniquely suited to do—if our economic activity is to contribute to the nurture, rest, and delight of the vast memberships we live among. If we are even moderately successful, we will make sure that production methods do not exhaust natural resources or degrade communities and workers, because then our enjoyment would come at the expense of another's misery. We will make every effort to honor the integrity and need of others by doing good, responsible work, work that brings practical, durable, and beautiful benefits to others. We will protect communities and habitats that are threatened by rapacious or violent economic practices, so that they too can enjoy peace and delight. As we do these things, we will have done much more than given 10 percent of our income to God. We will have given all our talents and energies to the great Sabbath goal: to facilitate creation's praise and thanksgiving to God.

A contemporary Sabbath economy will also have *the equitable distribution of resources* as a foremost goal. As the ancient Israelite model makes clear, "equitable distribution" does not mean that all people must enjoy the same or the same amount of goods. Uniformity is not the goal. What is crucial is that we be attentive to when we have enough and fully alert to when others do not have basic needs met. Just as the Israelites were aware that land (wealth) accumulation meant that others were pushed into states of deprivation and want, so we too must guard against the kinds of inequities that further diminish the capacities of others to live well.

This goal presupposes an economic accounting system that is transparent and comprehensive, a system that counts all the costs of our living and does not factor out as externalities the long-term expenses. We do not consider enough how personal wealth often comes at great cost to others and to natural habitats. Consider that the profitability of many corporations depends on low wages, inadequate employee benefits, lax safety controls, unchecked pollution, heavily subsidized raw materials, and the rape of natural (often publicly owned) lands. Or as was the case at the close of the last millennium, a tremendous disparity of income between executives and workers may be funded by the outsourcing of jobs to the lowest bidder, tax incentives (corporate welfare), and the curtailing or elimination of insurance and pension plans. The wealth of the few, much as in Egypt, is secured at the expense of the many.

Consider also the fact that in a consumer society such as our own, where individuals are mostly reduced to shoppers, we are all hugely ignorant about the products we buy, how they were made, and whether the workers who made them were justly compensated. The commodities we purchase have a sticker price that we are aware of, but the full costs are shrouded in mystery. Does the purchase of a new television, for instance, include the costs of heavy-metal mining practices and electric energy consumption, both of which wreak havoc with environments and rural and wilderness communities (think here of the devastation to ecosystems and towns brought on by mountaintop removal coal mining practices in Appalachia), or the costs associated with an old TV's now going into a landfill, where toxic elements eventually make their way into soils and groundwater networks?

In many instances we do not know the complete costs associated with our economic practices. As consumers we live in what Berry has called "the economy of the one-night stand":[5] we enjoy the good time associated with our consumption but prefer not to know the many details or histories of our products for fear that we might be ashamed of what we are doing. But if we are genuinely interested in a just and equitable economy, one that fosters *mutual* rest and delight, we need to know and honor these details and histories, the many layers of interdependence and cooperative membership. If we fail here, then it is naive to think that we have ordered our economic practices so that they reflect a Sabbath sensibility.

Keeping a Local Focus

Given the complexity and difficulty associated with knowing all the costs of our economic decisions—these having become even more obscure in our global economy—the ancient Israelites were wise to insist that *local production and need be the first priority.* Emphasizing and promoting local economies is important because then the loop between production and consumption does not get too long. The danger with a long loop, as we have already seen, is that it fosters mutual ignorance: buyers do not appreciate all that went into the production of a good, nor do producers know well or care for the contexts of consumers. The result is poorly made products in attempts to increase profitability and careless consumption as consumers do not fully value the costliness of what they consume. Moreover, a long loop makes it more likely that we will not see, live with, or correct the harmful effects of what we do.

Consider a simple example. Every week we put can upon can of garbage at the curb. Much of this waste results from the excessive packaging and slick advertising that are the inevitable result of a culture obsessed with "having" and "appearing." What is this waste? Is it dangerous or toxic? What will become of it when it leaves our curb? Why is there so much of it? These are questions we do not have to raise or answer, because we assume that someone else will take care of it. The garbage is out of sight and thus also out of mind. But what would happen if we had to deal with the garbage on our own? Would we refer to the dumpsite in our backyard as a "sanitary landfill"? Would we continue to buy products that promote excessive or dangerous amounts of waste? Or would we by stealth dump our waste on someone else's property and let them handle it? The fact of the matter is that in our economy we live by stealth more than we know. We don't want to think about all that is really involved in our production and consumption practices, because if we did we would quickly see that we are offloading serious problems—pollution, soil erosion, water contamination, unnecessary death, human disease connected to environmental despoliation, worker stress, and community disintegration—on distant people and unseen habitats.

The factors that have led to our collective irresponsibility are much the same for us as they were for the Israelites. Recall that this young nation sought the prestige of a king, believing that by having a king they would gain the respect and adulation of their neighbors. Though we may not be looking for a king today, we certainly still crave the respect, esteem, perhaps even awe, of our neighbors. To achieve our cravings we focus on abstract goals like wealth, a growing market, or rising stock prices, rather than on subsistence needs. Just as with the Israelites, the substitution of real goals—meeting the directly visible needs of local communities and families—with abstract ones means that we will sacrifice a great number of known goods for someone else's benefit.

This is exactly what happened in the 1990s. Thomas Frank has written in great detail about how in this period American culture as well as other countries around the world became obsessed with "market populism."[6]

Americans came to view the market in virtually divine terms, believing that it could solve social ills, increase democratic participation, fix environmental crises, and satisfy our every want. "The market" really meant a mad rush for some people to become as wealthy as quickly as possible. The watchword of the period was "Privatize, deregulate, and do not interfere with the market." The quests for market efficiency and expansion, most notably through transnational trade agreements and the World Trade Organization, made some individuals obscenely wealthy (in 1999 Bill Gates owned as much as 40 percent of the American population put together, while the assets of the world's top 358 billionaires equaled the combined income of the 2.3 billion poorest people!). At the same time, wealth polarization reached levels not seen in decades. Though productivity increased in the United States, worker wages either went down or remained stagnant. Meanwhile the natural and social resources we all need to live well—clean water, seed stock, intellectual "property," medical research, government by the people—went up for sale and became highly lucrative (for some).

When we become supporters of a local economy—purchasing food that is locally grown or products made by community members, investing in local financial cooperatives and small-scale currencies—what we do is elevate the subsistence needs of those in our community over the financial advantages of the unseen and unknown few. Sabbath people need to take the lead in practical ventures springing up around the country that support small businesses rather than the "big box" conglomerates that inevitably ruin locally run and locally owned enterprise. Though these big chains give us cheap goods, their cheapness reflects too many hidden costs that diminish creation's delight. As consumers we have the power to dramatically affect large-scale economic practices simply by choosing to spend our money differently, in ways that reward local initiative and energize neighborhood cohesion.[7] Studies have shown that money spent in support of locally owned and operated businesses generates almost twice the income for a local economy. So by investing in local projects and businesses, we will strengthen communities rather than weaken or erode them.

There are plenty of ways church people can take the lead. Because we profess to be a body and community united under the lordship of Christ, we should have built-in accountability networks that can help us share more with each other and spend less frivolously. There is no reason that we could not share the purchase and use of large-ticket items like tools and equipment or services like child and elder care. Surely we can be creative about how to hold things in common (Acts 2:44). The point, of course, is not to keep all goods for ourselves but also to make available to those in need clothing, household goods, and basic services like home repair. Moreover, churches themselves need to become wiser and more attentive in their shopping. Do we need to use all the paper we do or spray our lawns with so many poisons? Do we even need so much manicured lawn? A good alternative would be to convert some of our lawn space into a community garden where church members work together with the community to create beauty and cultivate wholesome food. And when we put on our dinners, churches could take the lead in buying from local organic farms, gardens, and CSAs (community-supported agriculture projects). In Hope CSA, for example, pastors and laypeople learn about sustainable food production, think theologically about it, and help to grow some of what they eat.[8] This would be a testimony to church members that how we eat matters, and it would be a help to the local food economy.

As we participate in local economies, we will position ourselves to become more honest and generous participants in God's economy. There are several dimensions to this honesty and generosity. On one level, we can take a more active role in the production of the things we need by refusing to be passive, ignorant consumers of products invisibly made. As we become involved in the production of goods, we begin to see more clearly the many costs and skills—energy, natural resources, traditional wisdom, practical intelligence, durable and beautiful design, and communal cooperation—associated with their goodness. Seeing directly the value of the natural and social sources that feed into our existence, we will be much less likely to degrade or abuse them.

On another level, we will become more neighborly and charitable because we will have a clearer view of the many layers of interdependence that make our lives possible. In the words of Berry: "In a viable neighborhood, neighbors ask themselves what they can do or provide for one another, and they find answers that they and their place can afford. This, and nothing else, is the *practice* of neighborhood. This practice must be, in part, charitable, but it must also be economic, and the economic part must be equitable; there is a significant charity in just prices."[9] A problem with our global economy is that prices, while often low, are hardly just because they contain many hidden costs to environments, communities, and personal health that will need to be picked up by someone else.

And on a third level, we will begin to appreciate the complexity and mystery of God's economy and become less brash and arrogant in our use of it. Today's industrial-technological economy assumes that we can easily have whatever we desire. And so we make economic decisions that have as their indirect consequence problems that are massive and extremely difficult to address. For example, we did not foresee that by applying millions of gallons of herbicide and fertilizer to stimulate agricultural production and suburban lawn growth we would in fact poison our water systems and produce massive "dead zones" in our oceans.

Often a technological solution gives rise to even larger problems that then must await yet more costly, and perhaps deadly, solutions. By focusing economic decision making on a smaller scale, we become more attentive to the limits and possibilities of particular places and communities, and through this patient attention we learn which solutions will do our biological and social neighborhoods the most long-term good.

To many of us the suggestion that we become proponents of local economies and subsistence production will sound ludicrous, especially given the global reach of economic practice today. We need to understand, however, what is really at stake. As numerous social theorists (including David Harvey, Anthony Giddens, and Zygmunt Bauman) have made clear, when we are swept up in a global economy we easily end up consenting to practices that render our relationships to habitats, regions, families, friends, and communities precarious, destructive, insecure, and superficial. This is because in a global marketplace what matters most are flexibility, speed, efficiency, and profitability. The frantic pace of our activity leaves no room for us to remember and honor God's generosity or to trust in his goodness. Ours is not the ideal context in which to develop Sabbath habits of attention, care, celebration, affection, loyalty, generosity, mercy, patience, and kindness. Yet these are precisely the habits to which God has been calling us since the beginning of time—habits that lead us into Sabbath rest and delight.

If we are to build something like a Sabbath economy, we must devise ways to extricate ourselves from current practices that lead to stress, exhaustion, injustice, and destruction so that we can better participate in God's ongoing care. Our security and peace do not reside in financial barons, marketing wizards, or globetrotting investors but in the face-to-face responsibility we demonstrate to each other. Only as we clearly see and patiently learn to appreciate the gifts of God that we are to each other will we develop the economic practices that foster mutual delight.

10

Sabbath Education

■ As a parent of four school-aged children, I consider their education with a good deal of anxiety. I am worried—not simply about inadequate buildings and schoolroom supplies, teacher and computer shortages, and declining standards. My major concern is how our educational systems are shaping my kids as people, as creatures made in the image of God. Education has become a stress-ridden enterprise in which parents and children alike jostle for the best schools and teachers, the highest grades, and the most beneficial (read "résumé-building") clubs and organizations. We think such jostling will give our kids access to better or more prestigious colleges and universities. And our anxiety does not end with college admission, because students then compete vigorously for the equally prestigious graduate and professional school or the lucrative (read "high-paying") firm or business. Even here, in the more settled routines of work life, our anxiety does not stop, as we contemplate moving up or moving on and make plans for the next generation of children to endure the same race.

Other parents I know share these same concerns. In our discussions, however, we rarely step out of the received paradigm to question its overall validity. More often than not our concern focuses on strategizing to beat the system so that we or our children can succeed despite its obstacles and shortcomings. We figure out ways to maneuver within our educational frameworks but do not really question the goals that keep the systems, however dysfunctional, going. Our collective anxiety and confusion demonstrate a profound inability to ask about what education is and what it is finally for.

Within mainstream culture, credentialing has taken priority over educating. What we crave is the degree, the well-padded résumé, because we view it as a ticket for a job interview and, having landed a job, entrance to the American dream. What we most fear is unemployment or the prospect of being unemployable. And so we devote a lot of time and personal resources, often acquiring significant financial debt along the way, to acquiring the credentials that will make us attractive to a prospective employer. As Jane Jacobs has observed, this arrangement is useful and highly profitable for human resources departments that do the hiring: "the institution of higher learning has done the tedious first winnowing or screening of applicants."[1] It is not, however, very beneficial to us, since it feeds upon and builds insecurity within us as we worry that we are not good enough or have not accomplished enough of public note.

Credentialing, besides leading to forms of social inequality and intensified personal anxiety, is inimical to education. When our focus is the standardized test or the degree and all that it might (we hope) deliver, we should not be surprised to hear teachers despair of students who seem "less interested in learning than in doing the minimum to get by and get out." Students, meanwhile, cannot help despairing of educational institutions that "think of them as raw material to process as efficiently as possible rather than as human beings with burning questions and confusions about the world and doubts about why they were sinking time and money into this prelude to their working lives."[2] Parents watch and lobby from the sidelines, hoping desperately that their kids will be among the ones who "make it" by gathering the most prestigious certifications. This is a frustrating position to be in. For some people, the only way out is to fake or embellish their test scores and accomplishments. For others—teachers, students, and administrators—who stay in the system, cynicism becomes the best available coping strategy.

Education as the Formation of Desire

To see how far we have moved away from something resembling a Christian view of education, we should ponder the words of Augustine: "The whole life of a good Christian is a holy desire." In the world of credentialing there is little room for a holy desire. Instead we find all manner of unholy pursuits and outcomes, such as the accumulation of personal prestige and wealth, the equating of personal freedom with purchasing power, the profitability of enterprises that degrade workers and natural environments alike, the erosion of family and communal life for the purposes of shareholder interests, the entrenchment of social stratification and division along educational lines, and the distortion of desire itself as people are reduced to buying machines more and more under the control of media and marketing moguls. The mind of the mature Augustine (one can read his *Confessions* as the journey toward a more holy desire), indeed the ethos of the early church, was profoundly different because it would endeavor to be faithful to a holy focus and purpose. Robert Wilken has summarized it by saying, "The Christian life was oriented toward a goal, toward life in fellowship with God. Its end was to know and love God as we have been known and loved by God, for only in knowing and loving God and sharing in God's life would human beings find happiness."[3] In what ways, we should ask, do our teaching and learning reflect our knowing, loving, *and sharing* in the life of God?

It is easy to dismiss this language of "fellowship with God" by making it abstract or merely pious in sentiment. To a large extent, this is what we have done in our own time when as church people we have consorted and made our peace with an economy "firmly founded on the seven deadly sins" (Berry). We do not see the incongruity between our consorting with prestige and profitability and our purported fellowship with God. Nor do we adequately appreciate how our educational machinery works hand in glove with industry and business to supply this economy with eager and devoted participants.

The early church linked our friendship with God to concrete daily practices, practices that had an educational core that has much to teach us. We need guidance in the ways of an authentic education, recognizing that without it we will not fully realize God's loving intentions for us. We need clarity about the overall aims of formal and informal education so that together we can form communities that will lead us into God's peace, justice, and joy. In short, we need to rethink education in terms of the Sabbath aspirations that founded and continue to propel all of creation.

A uniquely Sabbath sensibility, we have seen, develops as we learn to perceive and engage creation the way God does. Sabbath observance draws us into the grace of the world so that we can appreciate each other as creatures formed by an unfathomable divine love and goodness. When we welcome each other as gifts of God, we are positioned to share in the rest and delight, the *menuha*, that marked God's own *shabbat*, because now, for the first time, our anxious and prideful desires are transformed by God's celebratory and life-giving ways. The Sabbath is an invitation to experience each other and creation in their full depth as manifestations of God's own delight.

One way to think about our education is to see it as comprising multiple pathways in the exploration of this invitation to experience and welcome

131

each other as gifts of God. Sabbath education is concerned with inspiring, leading, and training people so that together we can more fully behold, understand, and celebrate the world as God's good creation and as divine blessings suited for our mutual well-being. Crucial to this whole enterprise is the formation of holy desires, attuned to God's intentions rather than our own. The transformation of our perception and desires is so vital because without it we run the risk of falsifying creation by reducing it to the scope of our own ambition or fancy, as when we degrade the sources of life to consumable commodities or debase each other to the level of pawns in the globalization game. Our most important educational task is to discover and take our fitting place within God's continuing life, so that our joy together can be made complete. Only then will we recognize the marks of well-educated persons to be not how many degrees they have or how much wealth and status they have acquired, but rather how well they contribute to the health and conviviality of our social and biological neighborhoods.

If we are to move in this Sabbath direction, we must begin with the practical aspects of the transformation of our desire. How does it happen, and what educational principles are involved? The psalmist pleads, "Create in me a clean heart, O God, and put a new and right spirit within me" (Ps. 51:10). For the biblical writers, as well as for the early church fathers and mothers, the transformation of desire begins with a conviction of our sinfulness, a realization that we are predisposed to cloud the gifts of God by turning them into possessions for our own narrowly conceived benefit. We do this crassly when, in full view of the poverty or deprivation of others, we selfishly appropriate more than we need. But we also do it subtly as career-driven professionals who care more about personal satisfaction than about the meeting of each other's and creation's deep needs. And so the psalmist continues by praying for a "broken spirit; a broken and contrite heart" (Ps. 51:17). Our most urgent need is to learn to engage each other with a clean heart, with a mind and will that has been purified of self-serving desires. Of course, such engagement presupposes that we face and speak honestly with each other, since we are notoriously incapable of seeing the sin in ourselves but able and willing to name the sins of others!

One way to characterize this educative process and goal is to see it as a faithful and honest attunement to the world, an apprenticeship to reality in which we gradually learn to distinguish between reality as God has given it to us and reality as we fancifully wish it to be. The image of apprenticeship is very illuminating because, besides having a venerable history as the preferred method of instruction in the arts of living, here we can see in a most mundane way the breaking of spirit the psalmist talks about. The new apprentice, a carpenter for instance, often begins with all kinds of expectations and illusions about how the craft of carpentry is best executed. But as work under the master teacher proceeds, the apprentice gradually comes to appreciate that attitude for the arrogance it is: a misinformed and potentially destructive (as in faulty or weak construction) imposition on the world. As apprentices, we begin to learn our craft only when we submit our mind and will to what the craft recommends: when we learn to work within the limits and possibilities of tools, building materials, artful and useful design, and social or communal priorities. We need to know what will work, what is strong and durable and aesthetically pleasing, what people need, and what natural habitats will sustainably allow. Only insofar as we line our work up with these possibilities and constraints and have put our mind and will in harmonious sympathy with them can we be said to have properly learned our craft.

We can describe this process as a breaking of the will because the apprentice has learned a more fitting and responsible (responsive to his or her context) focus, has become more attentive to the surrounding context, and has given up ambition to take the world by force. Narrow, selfish desire has been corrected and transformed into a desire for the health, beauty, and well-being (what the Bible refers to as salvation) of the communities in which we work and live. The apprentice becomes a master not by bending the world to his or her own will but by submitting to, learning to work within, and developing an affection for the rich possibilities latent within the craft. Of course, one's apprenticeship never comes to an end because there is always more to reality than was first thought. "There lives," as the poet Gerard Manley Hopkins observed in his poem "God's Grandeur," "the dearest freshness deep down things." We continue to learn throughout our lives as we open ourselves more and more to the potential and blessing present in each member of creation.

Current educational priorities diverge radically from this apprenticeship perspective. For the most part, our educational aspirations have a self-serving focus that encourages us to disregard the particular needs of the place we live in, given the need to "grow the economy," even if that means destroying or degrading local habitats and communities. Eric Zencey has accurately described this sort of education as "rootless," because it has as its expressed aim the production of cosmopolitan individuals (consumers) who have little or no allegiance to a local community or geographical territory. Shunning such fidelity as parochial or provincial, teachers encourage young people "to abjure their citizenship in the political, biotic, and familial communities of their nativity and to embrace citizenship in the world city of ideas and culture [and commerce, we should add]."[4] Students reject, or even learn to despise, immediate connections to place and neighborhood in favor of the less demanding connections to an abstract world of ambition and progress. In this context of rootlessness and fanciful projection ample opportunity exists for self-glorification and for the destruction of our created homes.

Rootlessness leads to the dismemberment of the mind and of creation. Consider the fact that in our information and technological age, when we purportedly have more knowledge than ever before, we are witnesses to and agents of the most widespread ecological destruction and communal disintegration the world has ever known. Something is desperately wrong with an educational system that does not adequately prepare us to consider, address, and learn the basic skills of our life together, that does not teach us in the arts of conservation, protection, celebration, and maintenance. Though we may produce remarkable communicators (often communicating little of value) or efficient managers (often managing sites that are exhausted or degraded), the fact of the matter is that current education does precious little to develop in us the basic competencies of life—growing and preparing food, raising a family, judging quality, maintaining a home, practicing hospitality, or making a toy—that are vital and indispensable to a healthy and successful life. Because many of our educational agendas are driven by "the career of money," most basically in the form of corporate funding and in the promotion of the most lucrative (especially to corporations) fields of study, we should not be surprised that the most essential skill graduates must learn is how to write a check or lay down a credit card. Education, rather than leading us into freedom, fosters various forms of bondage as we move further into economic debt (beginning with our educational costs!) owing to our collective ignorance and incompetence.

Our rootlessness, in other words, leads us to neglect precisely those elements in life that are essential and fundamental. In the name of civilization and culture, we learn to despise the agriculture and aquaculture that are necessarily—at least insofar as we eat and drink—their root. In the name of upward mobility, we readily abandon the communities that gave us, however inadequately, a home and a sense of direction. Our departure contributes to a steady drain on small communities and is a boon to large urban centers that find in the fleeing hordes a captive and largely helpless workforce. In the name of sophistication, we shun the insights of traditional wisdom, characterizing them as old-fashioned and out-of-date. Of course this hubris is greatly encouraged by the profiteers who stand to make considerable income from the practical witlessness we display. Having forsaken the competencies that accumulate over long histories of trial and error, and having been reduced to consumers, we have little choice but to pay handsomely for performance of all the tasks we are unable to perform ourselves. This is not only a disconnection of our mind from our hands and feet (and the skills they should be taught to perform) but also a dismemberment from each other and our past and the wisdom we could have drawn from it.

Education into Wholeness

A better way is to conceive education as our initiation into wholeness. To be sure, there is a sense in which our "wholeness" will remain preliminary and imperfect owing to the divisive and alienating character of our sinful lives. We live in a broken and wounded world and in a culture that encourages isolation and fragmentation. But from a practical standpoint, the desire for wholeness means that we make our local community and habitat, the native network of relationships that directly feed and nurture us, the focus of sustained attention and study. This is not so that we can avoid what is foreign, different, or exotic. It is rather so that we can see more clearly and understand with greater honesty the requirements, limits, and potential of our life together. It is so that we can become fully attentive to our concrete situation, celebrate the gifts that we are to each other, and take responsibility for our collective needs.

The danger of avoiding the realities and constraints of our native homes is that our perceiving, thinking, and willing will become abstract and naively unrealistic as we substitute the truths of our life with our ambitious and fanciful projections. That colleges and universities have fallen into this trap is readily seen in the fact that serious teaching, the sort that entails many face-to-face hours between student and teacher, has been eclipsed by the drive to improve rankings by increasing research production through corporate and government funding. It is often unclear how such research actually improves our communities or benefits our citizens.

Put simply and directly, we need to think about education in more *ecological* terms. Ecology is the science of relationships, the study of how the various members of our life together do not and cannot function alone but rely on multiple layers of influence and nurture to be what they are. It is a tool to help us understand the dynamics of interdependent wholeness. Education can be our primary means for seeing wholeness if we can learn to resist the hyperspecialization that plagues our curricula. As specialists who study very limited sections of the spectrum of life, we are unable to appreciate how our narrow learning grows out of and affects the larger reality. Students routinely claim that they do not see how what they learn in biology has anything to do with what they learn in a literature or religion class. This is a travesty: it means that we who are teachers have failed to communicate the wholeness of life or the fact that our lives are benefited in countless, often unseen ways by a diverse and vast neighborhood of human and nonhuman memberships, and that what we do in turn also has multiple, unforeseen effects on a multitude of others. Having erred on this score, we prepare our young generations for an even greater failure: the failure of responsibility for our life together.

We cannot develop as responsible members of communities and habitats if we do not adequately see and appreciate the many patterns of interdependence and influence everywhere at work. Education that is focused on initiating us into wholeness will make apparent the connections between human ill-health and degraded or toxic soils and watersheds, between worker anxiety and global economics, between social and personal boredom and the entertainment and marketing industries, between ephemeral faith and consumer culture. Only as we see these connections can we be in a position to make the changes that are necessary to correct our many social and environmental problems. We cannot expect to produce whole human beings, people who live knowledgeably and appropriately—with a sense of propriety and modesty—within multiple networks of relationships, if the educational system we run them through is characterized by fragmentation and excessive specialization.

Another way to state this is to suggest that education must become one of the primary means for overcoming the distance and misunderstanding that prevent us from entering into faithful and honest relationships with each other. In this respect the main temptation educators need to avoid is not simply hyperspecialization but the climate of suspicion and doubt that now passes as the default methodology in our study and our classrooms. Obviously, history gives us many reasons to be legitimately suspicious of institutionalized and officially sanctioned forms of power. But in our desire to be critical we have simply become cynical. The cool, unaffected posture of would-be intellectuals leads to lives devoid of commitment and care. It eventually leads to our collective abandonment of the world and of each other. It is a striking condemnation of existing educational frameworks that for all our talk about developing critical, reflective abilities in our students we are, as a group, remarkably passive and unable—or unwilling—to critically question and change the destructive patterns of our current economic and political situation.

Embracing the World

We would do better if we followed Susan Felch's advice to practice a "hermeneutics of delight" and not only a hermeneutics of suspicion. Her reason is simple: excessive doubt prevents us from fully entering into the world. As she puts it, when doubt is reified and hardened, what we get is a flattened aesthetic and moral landscape, in which the rich diversity of human experience is reduced to the single mode of questioning and interrogation and the wide range of possible moral response is reduced to modes of distance and distrust. In this respect doubt obscures, rather than clarifies, our vision. Delight, on the other hand, opens our faculties to the rich plenitude of creation. As a hermeneutic or method of interpretation, it encourages us to "look up and around" and to loosen the "constricted pathways of precept and rule" so that we can more spontaneously and more freshly engage each other. Surely at the heart of all our knowing there must be the recognition that there is always more to know and that our purported understanding is always laced with great ignorance and lack. When we practice the hermeneutics of delight, we will put ourselves into a more honest position as learners, not because we have forsaken all critical doubt but because we have opened ourselves to the mystery and grace of God and made ourselves available to share in, be responsible for, and enjoy the embodied love that creation itself is.[5]

A good practical place to begin as we move toward a hermeneutic of delight is to greatly restrict the use of computer technologies in our classrooms, especially among the young. Educators of computer literacy tell us that the computer skills we most need (in the adult world, presumably) can readily be taught in one year at the high school level. Starting earlier, besides being very expensive for school systems (though profitable to providers), has the potential to do considerable harm to our young people.

The harm I am talking about takes several forms. One is the loss of wonder in and appreciation for the ordinary, necessary processes of natural life. Children today commonly find the movements of butterflies and bees, or the work of earthworms, intolerably unexciting or dull when compared to the speed and explosiveness of simulated war games, even though bees and worms perform services indispensable for the continuation of life. Further, the safety and relative ease of an electronic buffer allows "relationships" with foreigners around the world while we ignore and in some cases fear the foreigner in our midst. Even more important is the loss of a sense of a larger world that far exceeds our comprehension and control, a world that is wild and not simply the mere extension of our desire. A whole generation of young people is growing up with the assumption that their world should be available "on demand" and subject to their complete control; media programming can be enjoyed on their own terms, as when viewers fast-forward through a TV drama and thus avoid the little subtlety or complexity that they might meet. Educators need to work very hard to resist the superficiality and hyperbole of electronic media, because as creatures of God we define who we are by encountering and learning to relate to a world that is not us and that does not exist on our terms. We need to encounter as deeply and directly as possible the miraculous character of our lives together. When we lose the sense that life is indeed a miracle, it is much more likely that we will abuse it.

Computer technology plays an important role in the erosion of our sense of wonder because it intoxicates us with the possibility for a completely controlled life. Recent technologies have put the world at our fingertips. We can access, manipulate, and redesign reality with a few keystrokes. If we want a sound, an image, or a relationship, all we need to do is type it in. Then, if what we have received is not satisfactory or pleasing, we can simply change it or exit the program. This gives people tremendous power over the reality they engage.

Clearly education is about empowerment, but it is not this sort of power that we should be encouraging. For starters, the power we have through computers is the power a computer technician or programmer has made possible. It is packaged power that is decided upon by someone else. It is also lazy power, because children can now perform tasks that would otherwise take the development of considerable skill and patience. Failing this development, we also forfeit the internal discipline and social cooperation that went with the learning of a particular skill. For instance, when a student can use a program to construct a structure or essay, the program will compensate for errors in judgment by correcting mistakes automatically. The student is deprived of a most important lesson—that our power and knowledge are susceptible to disastrous effects and that we need to learn through our mistakes.

In short, computer technologies are dangerous because they give rise to a manipulative and arrogant disposition within us. As Lowell Monke puts it,

> The very idea of the dignity of a subject evaporates when everything becomes an object to be taken apart, reassembled or deleted. . . . The computer environment attracts children exactly because it strips away the very resistance to their will that so frustrates them in their concrete existence. Yet in the real world, it is precisely an object's resistance to unlimited manipulation that forces a child (or anyone) to acknowledge the physical limitations of the natural world, the limits of one's power over it, and the need to respect the will of others living in it.[6]

Life is not something we can control with a mouse. It cannot be contained within a computer program except in severely reduced and distorted form. If we want to do our children a service, we would do best to teach them that the world is an inexhaustible fountain of surprise and blessing and that to be responsible citizens within the world they need to become aware that the acquisition of power must be preceded by a moral preparation that enables them to wield it with discernment and with the objective of care and respect.

The school program advocated by Maria Montessori makes much Sabbath sense, since it encourages children to explore the world directly and creatively, with an eye to its rich depth and complexity. Rather than being limited to what a computer allows or doesn't, children need the freedom of time and space to see how their lives fit within the wider world and how reality often resists and exceeds—because of its profundity and mystery—whatever we might want to make of it. As students are encouraged to develop their imaginative and sympathetic faculties, they will come to appreciate better and in more detail how human life is lived best not when we control and manipulate each other but when we welcome each other with respect and care.

The Montessori approach creates a learning environment in which students, starting at the ages of three and four, can respond spontaneously and creatively to whatever they encounter. Adults do not give in prepackaged form the "learning" they are to achieve, nor do they impose a regimented or rigid schedule on the flow of learning. Rather, personal discovery is encouraged as students encounter and explore the rich reality of the world. Independent exploration, a nonuniform pace, and an emphasis on personal creativity encourage precisely the sort of wonder in our world that Albert Einstein feared was being systematically killed by formal education.

Another example of how students can be drawn into the rich depth and wonder of the world is Alice Waters's Edible Schoolyard program in California. Waters, a world-renowned chef who for years has been serving fresh, locally grown organic foods in her restaurant Chez Panisse, noticed that students needed to develop a close, complex relationship with their environment and their food. She began by turning a middle-school asphalt lot into a one-acre garden. Classrooms and curricula have since developed around the experience of students' growing, preparing, serving, and then eating their own food. In this program students learn lessons of stewardship, nutrition, and etiquette but also economics, biology, and geography. They learn how to work together and in sympathetic attunement to the limits and potential of natural rhythms. This is teaching and learning that takes the depth and mystery of creation seriously and that helps us overcome the notion that we can control each other and the world at will.

It should be clear by now that Sabbath education, training us in the ways of a holy desire, has the transformation of vision as its indispensable and continuing aim. What we most need is to find the ways that will help us *see* with depth and precision the details of our interconnected life with each other. Only then will we be able to discern how we are blessed by the presence and influence of others and how we in turn can be a blessing to them. This will not be easy, and not simply because there are, as I have already mentioned, multiple institutional, educational obstacles. There is yet another impediment to true learning, an impediment that, strangely and somewhat paradoxically, is linked with the desire to know itself.

We generally take for granted that the desire to understand or know is innocent. This is a mistake, however, because for people formed by the witness of scripture it should be plain that we are not innocent and that a controlling, even rapacious desire can motivate our best efforts. The story of the Israelites' wandering (and wondering?) in the wilderness needs to stand ever before us as a reminder of our own hubris and sin. The quest for knowledge is rarely, if ever, purely disinterested. For this reason we need to be especially attentive to the quest for knowledge itself. Or as Simone Weil would have put it, we need to be more attentive to the faculty of attention.

In her famous essay "Reflections on the Right Use of School Studies with a View to the Love of God" Weil observes: "We do not obtain the most precious gifts by going in search of them but by waiting for them. Man cannot discover them by his own powers, and if he sets out to seek for them he will find in their place counterfeits of which he will be unable to discern the falsity."[7] The problem with setting out in search of things and with our desire to know is that the inclinations of the ego readily come between ourselves and what we desire to know. We don't really make genuine contact with the world outside of us because we are always running into our own ambition or fear, our own desires and worries. As Weil puts it, "The imagination is continually at work filling up all the fissures through which grace might pass."[8]

If we are to meet God's grace and be transformed by it, we will have to learn to subdue our ego and get it out of the way so that a more direct approach to reality is possible. We need to confront and correct our propensity to reduce others to the satisfaction of our own desires. When we learn to quell the ravenous ego through practices of confession and repentance, we become available to receive the gifts of God as genuine gifts rather than as possessions. We learn, as it were, to get ourselves out of the line of sight. The point is not to detach ourselves from the world and from each other but to detach from ourselves because we often get in the way of a genuine encounter. Detachment of this sort will enable education to contribute to the clarification of vocation in our lives.

In talking about self-detachment we can go to extremes of self-hatred—a charge often raised against Weil herself. This is why it is important to be honest about how we attend to ourselves as well as to others. True attention, the sort that leads to a clear and faithful embrace of each other, is always informed by love. We come to see others as the expression of divine love and as deserving our care, just as we come to see ourselves as equally borne and sustained by love. This is what genuine humility is, "knowing that in what we call 'I' there is no source of energy by which we can rise."[9] The energy that "helps us rise" and move at all always comes from others, most notably the divine Other. Authentic education, which I could here describe as a learned humility, will encourage us to acknowledge and respect that others help us rise. It will also propel us to act responsibly within our interdependent wholeness. Attentive love is the path that leads us into the intimacy that makes delight possible. Indeed, "the only organ of contact with existence is acceptance, love. That is why beauty and reality are identical. That is why joy and the sense of reality are identical."[10]

Sabbath education is education that equips us to be honest and merciful so that we can face each other and ourselves as what we are: concrete expressions of the love of God. That we do not care for or celebrate each other enough, and that we do not sufficiently attend to the brokenness evident in our world, is a mark of our blindness and sinfulness. As Sabbath people, we will therefore need to promote instruction in and occasions for the practice of forgiveness, so that our desire can become a holy one that shares in the life-sustaining, celebratory ways of God. If we are to learn the practice of delight, we must practice the arts of welcome and nurture, of reconciliation and healing, for it is only then that we will be able to stand before each other and before God with the knowledge that our lives have been devoted to the flourishing of all. Our Sabbath education is a school of conversion and celebration in which our collective anxieties, fears, and arrogance are transformed into humility, awe, and delight.

11

Sabbath Environmentalism

■ That the Sabbath completes and is intended for the whole of creation is likely one of the least appreciated aspects of Sabbath teaching. The fact that it is underappreciated is an important clue that we are still a long way from being the people God ultimately wants us to be. When we think about the Sabbath, its scope and concern are almost always reduced to a human level. This clearly will not suffice, particularly if we recognize that the experience of *menuha* presupposes a winnowing of self-obsessed ambitions so that the intentions of God for all can be realized. Sabbath teaching confronts head on, and then corrects, the anthropocentric assumptions within us, assumptions that lead us to believe that finally the human realm is of sole importance. From a Sabbath point of view, however, the range of God's concern and delight is all-encompassing.

The wide dimensions of Sabbath teaching are mostly lost on us because, as modern urbanites, we have little appreciation for the world as God's creation. We do not appreciate it as the material, mundane domain through which the grace of God is made manifest. We are, in multiple ways, shielded from and thus largely ignorant about our dependencies on God and the created order. We do not, except on rare (generally catastrophic) occasions, have to think about where energy comes from, if the water we drink and the air we breathe are clean and readily available, or if the materials we need for work—ranging from wood to hemp to iron to fossil fuel to minerals to cotton—are sustainably harvested and justly distributed. Having been reduced to the status of consumers, to people who have little if any sustained contact with the processes of creation, we assume that whatever we need we can invent ourselves or purchase at the store. The result is that we live in a world mostly of our own rather than God's making. We have, as our living suggests, ceased to think of ourselves as creatures and have proclaimed ourselves to be gods. Practically speaking, there is really very little for which to express to God our thanks and praise. As masters of the earth and of our own fate, we can thank ourselves. Creation does not figure into our thinking about the Sabbath because it does not factor much into our thinking about us.

Our denial of creation leads to serious distortions in how we understand a properly human life. The first, most fundamental truth about us is that we are not our own but are creatures enmeshed in the lives of the rest of creation—all dependent upon God. Since creation is God's love made manifest and concrete—in the forms of birth and growth, decomposition and fertility, respiration and digestion, healing and vitality—insofar as we are cut off from creation we are significantly cut off from God's action in the world. Thomas Aquinas reasoned that as God is the "cause" of creatures (because God creates *ex nihilo* or "from nothing," we simply cannot comprehend the mechanics of divine causation), and given that "existence is more intimately and profoundly interior to things than anything else . . . God must exist and exist intimately in everything" (*Summa Theologica* 1a8.1). When we turn our backs on creation, we turn against God. Again, Thomas put the point plainly: "Any error about creation also leads to an error about God" (*Summa contra Gentiles* 2.3).

The wide scope of our contemporary environmental crisis—massive soil erosion, water degradation and depletion, global warming, air pollution, coastal degradation, species extinction, deforestation, desertification, and habitat destruction and loss—indicates that we have erred dramatically in our treatment of the gift of God's creation. We have to assume, given the extent of this destruction and Christendom's complicity in the plan "to murder creation" (Berry), that we are in the midst of a catastrophic error about who we understand God to be and what we think God expects of us. We have failed in our Christian discipleship, particularly if we mean by discipleship the making manifest of "that courtesy to creatures in which reverence for the Creator finds expression."[1]

Understanding Creation

A significant source of our error about creation, and thus also God, is that we fail to see the whole world *as God's creation*. We have been trained to think that there is a physical world out there called "nature," maybe even Mother Nature, and that it is our job to use it as we see fit. The term *nature*, however, is not a biblical one. The Bible nowhere assumes a natural, ungraced world that exists entirely on its own. To be sure, God extends to creation a measure of independence and creativity so that it can develop in new ways. But the world is what it is because of the charitable and hospitable action of God. It depends on God for its continuing existence from moment to moment; notions of God's interfering "from outside" are mistaken.[2]

Psalm 65 beautifully describes God's intimate involvement in the ways of creation's fecundity. This is the occasion for the psalmist's continuing song of praise; the whole psalm is one long act of adoration in which God's and the psalmist's delight in creation's beauty are expressed:

> You visit the earth and water it,
>   you greatly enrich it;
> the river of God is full of water;
>   you provide the people with grain,
>   for so you have prepared it.
> You water its furrows abundantly,
>   settling its ridges,
> softening it with showers,
>   and blessing its growth.
> You crown the year with your bounty;
>   your wagon tracks overflow with richness.
> The pastures of the wilderness overflow,
>   the hills gird themselves with joy,
> the meadows clothe themselves with flocks,
>   the valleys deck themselves with grain,
>   they shout and sing together for joy.
>
> (Ps. 65:9–13)

This psalm sings the biblical refrain that without God we are nothing. God's commitment to love the world into vitality gives rise to creation's spontaneous joy and praise to God (cf. Isa. 55:12). God is forever near us, in the intimacy of our own breath and as the energy and life that keeps creation on the move. When we think we don't need God anymore or believe that we can go it alone, we fall into error and join the ranks of the wicked. To be a sinful dullard is to think that we can secure life on our own terms and through our own (often violent or destructive) cunning and might.

As the biblical witness makes clear, our practical living amongst *all* the members of creation is a deeply religious matter. This point needs stressing, especially in an age of individualism, because we are tempted to think that religious faith is ultimately and primarily about the believer's personal relation to God and then secondly about how we humans treat and relate to each other. Faith is thus reduced to a spiritual affair that does not have a lot to do with bodies. The danger of a disembodied or gnostic faith, besides denying the incarnation of God in flesh, is that it becomes nearly inevitable that we will devalue and forget the many other bodies of creation too. When we fully admit the body into religious life, we are at the same time compelled to think about and care for other bodies—microorganisms, earthworms, tomatoes, wheat, bees, chickens—because it is through them that our living takes place. Our bodies, in other words, join us integrally to the whole of creation and thus also to the life of God there at work.

While it is proper to make distinctions between our body and our soul, we must never forget, as Wendell Berry has noted, that we are always and necessarily "caught in a network of mutual dependence and influence that is the substantiation of their unity. Body, soul (or mind and spirit), community, and world are all susceptible to each other's influence, and they are all conductors of each other's influence. The body is damaged by the bewilderment of the spirit [a bewilderment often caused by its inattentiveness to the body], and it conducts the influence of that bewilderment into the earth, the earth conducts it into the community, and so on."[3] Given these many layers of interdependence, how dishonest and foolish it is to say that we love God but then fail to love our brothers and sisters *and* their bodies and the bodies of all creation.

There is an inexorable logic at work in the Sabbath that will not allow us to separate ourselves from the rest of creation and the creation from God. For as soon as we make our separation, we condemn ourselves to loneliness and creation to violence. The health of our bodies is necessarily and beneficially tied to the health of the bodies of creation. Again, Berry has made this point clearly: "The willingness to abuse other bodies is the willingness to abuse one's own. To damage the earth is to damage your children. To despise the ground is to despise its fruit; to despise the fruit is to despise its eaters."[4] To this we need only add, to despise the creation is also to despise—no matter what our mouths may proclaim—God as its Creator.

To help us appreciate our membership within creation, the Sabbath code was very clear about not restricting Sabbath observance to humans alone. Consider the teaching about the Sabbath year: "For six years you shall sow your land and gather in its yield; but the seventh year you shall let it rest and lie fallow, so that the poor of your people may eat; and what they leave the wild animals may eat. You shall do the same with your vineyard, and with your olive orchard" (Exod. 23:10–11). Leviticus 25:3–7 makes a similar statement:

> Six years you shall sow your field . . . but in the seventh year there shall be a sabbath of complete rest for the land, a sabbath for the LORD: you shall not

sow your field or prune your vineyard. You shall not reap the aftergrowth of your harvest or gather the grapes of your unpruned vine: it shall be a year of complete rest for the land. You may eat what the land yields during its sabbath—you, your male and female slaves, your hired and your bound laborers who live with you; for your livestock also, and for the wild animals in your land all its yield shall be for food.

Here we find roughly parallel requirements for the provision of food, as well as rest, for humans and nonhumans alike. Our Sabbath rest must not be at the expense of another's toil or misery; we must exercise care to make sure that the alien and the household servant, but also animals and the land itself, are properly nourished and cared for.

When understood within the agricultural context of ancient Israelite life, this message is a ringing reminder that we depend on each other for our own well-being and that to damage creation is at the same time to damage ourselves. We need good work to make it through life, but we also need healthy animals and vibrant land in which all our living can be done. The protection and rest of land and animals thus become a major concern.

The history of North American land settlement and management practices suggests that we have seriously distorted the concept of being stewards of creation. The key biblical text here is Genesis 1:28, where God tells Adam and Eve to "be fruitful and multiply, and fill the earth and subdue it; and have dominion over the fish of the sea and over the birds of the air and over every living thing that moves upon the earth." This command to have dominion over creation has taken on a life of its own, becoming separated from biblical notions of dominion. For instance, in a technological world like our own, where we have the capacity to alter the genetic makeup of living organisms and the power of machines to blast, burn, and remove whole mountains, "dominion" can easily result in the dramatic alteration of creation's integrity and our redesigning creatures and habitats to suit narrow, merely profitable objectives. Dominion thus comes to be expressed through violence and brute force, with little or no heed paid to the scriptural proviso that our dominion, to be authentic, must be an outgrowth of our being the image of God and thus must engage creation in a way that mirrors God's own creative power. Nor does it bear much relation to the dominion displayed by Jesus Christ, who is Lord and Master over heaven and earth. What we see in him is a power that works transformatively and cooperatively rather than by violence. The power of Christ is a servant power that attends to the needs of those in his charge. It is a dominion that results in the healing and strengthening of those served because a servant is one who puts the needs of others at the forefront.

Since we obviously do have tremendous power over creation, the most important consideration for us is whether we will learn to become stewards who "subdue and dominate" by force or by service. Environmental history shows that attempts to dominate by force, and in wanton disregard of ecosystem processes, are doomed to failure. As numerous works of historical analysis have shown, Jared Diamond's *Collapse: How Societies Choose to Fail or Succeed* being one among them, whole civilizations can come to ruin if they despise the environmental contexts upon which every culture is built. If we are going to live out our dominion in a biblical way, a way that honors our membership within creation, we are going to need to recover some of the agrarian principles that informed the biblical writers.

Sabbath Environmental Principles

Among these principles, one of the most important is an attentive regard for our memberships. We need a detailed understanding of how our living intersects in multiple ways with human and nonhuman others, and then we must make sure that these intersections of influence are protected and made sustainable. Put another way, we need to enlarge the contexts or frames of reference we use when we make our decisions.

Consider how we use water. For the most part our reflection goes no further than the faucet or spigot. We don't consider how freshwater sources, whether in the aboveground forms of streams, rivers, lakes, snowpacks, and glaciers or underground aquifers (only some of which are replenishable), are in many areas on the verge of collapse or exhaustion owing to agricultural and industrial uses. We don't think about how diet decisions directly affect the availability of water. If we did, we would realize that meat protein (especially the varieties raised in large confinement operations), followed by the irrigation of grain crops that feed the animals and us (often inefficiently), use many hundreds of times the amount of water we directly drink. Nor are we aware of how the unavailability of water in many parts of the world, especially in a time of rapid population growth, will contribute to political unrest, the creation of massive refugee populations, and the destabilization of world markets. If we truly care about the well-being of all God's creatures, then we need to learn how the members of creation connect in more ways than we might first think. We all—soil, plants, animals, and people—need water.

As consumers we simply need to become much more attentive to how consumer choices affect the livelihood of countless seen and unseen creatures. As ecologists like to remind us, everything connects, and there is no free lunch. We can never do only one thing, because the effects of our actions extend far beyond our current place and time. When we fail to be attentive—most often because we let economic ambition or cheap prices override the dictates of care—we will quickly render our lands and animals exhausted and sick. But as we exercise proper care and restraint, we will discover that we can live together in sustainable, even convivial relationships. The precondition, however, is that our stewardship take a posture of servant care and respect. As servants we better acknowledge and live out our interdependence and memberships with each other. Human power is transformed by God's life-giving power so that others can flourish. The mark of the servant is that he or she suspends personal ambition so that the membership of creation can be nurtured and strengthened. This sort of stewardship makes genuine celebration that affirms the rights of creatures to be and to flourish possible, because it is no longer premised on the exhaustion or abuse of creation.

The rabbis understood this, and that is why they felt it important to impose restrictions on human economic activity. In the Talmud, for instance, the rabbis pondered the command to let the land lie fallow on every seventh year, to leave it alone so that it can rest and the animals have access to its fruit. Their practical conclusion was that if the spirit of the command is to be truly followed, the fences that mark personal ownership and bar common access to humans and animals must be torn down. This dramatic action is a potent symbol attesting to the fact that finally the land is not a personal possession that we can do with as we please. The land, as we have seen in a previous chapter, is God's, and is given as a common membership to the benefit of all. In order for us to appreciate this membership, come to respect and even celebrate it, we need regular reminders telling us that in our economic pursuits we are often far too presumptuous. Having in place legislation like the Sabbath year ensures that human dominion and ambition will find the necessary restrictions that will finally keep us from destroying our natural habitats and, by implication, ourselves.

There is still more to learn from the rabbis, for it is not enough that we tear down our fences. We must also, from time to time, change the methods whereby we extract the fruit of creation. Consider the curious formulation of Leviticus 25:5–6, where we are told not to reap or gather the harvest or vine *and* that we are to "eat what the land yields during its sabbath." How shall we eat without reaping or gathering? On the rabbinic view, this passage is telling us that we must not gather in the customary manner that makes use of technologically efficient methods. We can harvest, but not in ways that allow us to maximize production or benefit for ourselves. By curtailing our extractive ingenuity—by minimizing the use of even primitive tools—we enter into a simpler and more humble relationship with the land. We learn to distinguish between what we need and what we want, between a necessity and a luxury. Though we might have the technology and skill to increase production or accumulate wealth, this command teaches us to recognize that our ambition and skill are not the proper measure of healthy relationships in creation. The legitimacy of the economies and markets we devise, which so obviously lead to stress and destruction, is thus judged by the creative and vital rhythms of God's own economy.

Rabbinic teaching continued by noting that food harvested in the Sabbath year could be eaten but not used for commercial purposes or personal profit. Again, the practical significance of this command should not be underestimated. The restrictions on commercial transactions aim to limit what we do with the land to its "natural use" rather than its economic potential. When fruits of the earth are taken out of the realm of business (and largely human-focused) transactions, the possibility is restored that we will come to see the produce of the earth as God's gift. The fruit of the earth, in this command, is not to be converted into money to be hoarded, invested, or spent on nonessential pursuits.

The climax of these Sabbath year commands, however, comes when we are told that the yield of the land is for domestic *and* wild animals. According to the rabbis, this means that people are free to feed themselves and their domestic animals from the harvest they have gathered and stored up. But the moment there is not enough food in the wild—"God's natural storage"—for wild animals, then people must release food from their granaries and make it available to them. Gerald Blidstein summarizes this command well: "Man must relinquish that which his human capabilities have achieved, and in his use of the growth of the soil be reduced to the lowest of creatures that live off the soil. Man must live the rhythms of nature, despite his obvious ability and duty to circumvent them; he must live the rhythms of the countryside despite the city in which he dwells."[5] This is a clear and practical statement of what servant stewardship looks like: forgoing one's privilege so that the membership of which one is a part can be kept whole and healthy. To be a servant of creation is to seek to live according to its rhythms and in sympathetic alignment with its potential but also its limits.

Living Creation's Rhythms

It is relatively easy at this point to dismiss these rabbinic strictures as outdated and utterly impractical. After all, very few of us live on the land or are in a position to live close to its rhythms and needs. What could we possibly do that would do justice to the spirit of these commands?

One of the most important things for us to do is to make a detailed consumer inventory. Making such an inventory involves examining as precisely as we can where the things we buy come from and how they were produced and evaluating personal shopping patterns. A little research will quickly show that many consumer products are made in ways that take a very destructive toll on our environments.

Consider the burgeoning bottled-water industry. Bottled-water consumption is growing yearly at a worldwide rate of 12 percent and at a total cost to consumers of about thirty-five billion dollars. A significant impetus behind this development is water scarcity and water degradation—but also the lure of corporate profitability. Underground aquifers have been severely depleted, rivers and streams have been siphoned until they run dry or are polluted by agricultural runoff and industrial waste, while snowcaps and glaciers have diminished in size due to global warming. Further, to bottle now scarce fresh water, massive amounts of plastic need to be produced. But to make one kilogram of this plastic, 17.5 kilograms of water are used in a manufacturing process that emits 40 grams of hydrocarbons, 25 grams of sulfur oxides, 18 grams of carbon monoxide, 20 grams of nitrogen oxides, and 2.3 kilograms of carbon dioxide (a major source of greenhouse warming gases). Then add the fuel costs of transportation and distribution and the costs associated with landfills because many of these bottles are not recycled.[6]

If we were serious about being responsible stewards of creation, we would count all these costs and see that they are not worth it. We would be much wiser if we transferred our energy and consumer investments to preventing agricultural and industrial pollutants in the first place, and thus render our tap water safe to drink. (Studies have already shown that bottled water is often less pure than the tap water in our homes.) We would lobby and be willing to pay for more efficient use of water resources in industry and agriculture. We would drive less and conserve more energy because automobiles and coal-fired electricity-generating plants are major contributors to global warming. If we did these things, we would also have to stop buying industrial food and other products that are highly processed and made with toxic or fossil-fuel components. We would buy more organic food and locally produced goods. As the demand for responsibly produced and harvested goods rises, companies that are abusive of the environment will have to either change their production practices or go out of business. All of this we can do, even as urbanite shoppers, provided we take the time to be attentive to where our shopping dollars go. We can gradually bring ourselves into a healthier and more sympathetic alignment with the ways of creation if we commit ourselves to broadening and deepening our vision and expanding our frames of reference.

Scientists and researchers tell us that human activity—mostly related to our consumption patterns—is tragically out of step with what creation can afford. We are already mining, using up, wasting, or destroying the gifts of God at a rate that ecosystems cannot keep up, just as China's and India's massive economies are becoming westernized in their consumption patterns. Creation's tragedy is compounded by the fact that the nations most formed by a biblical ethos—those in North America and Europe—while having a modest 11 percent of the world's population, are responsible for 60 percent of the world's consumer expenditures. These expenditures are not going toward the healing of creation's memberships but to the satisfaction of personal ambition and comfort. If we are to become Sabbath people who take a humble stance within creation, who recognize creation as a gift of God given for all to enjoy, we simply have to realign and dramatically curtail our consumption habits.

It is important to realize that we will not be able to do this easily as individuals. Sabbath practices are corporate in nature, which means that we will need to enlist the help of others to keep us accountable and true to our better intentions. Could we not gather as friends who commit ourselves to help each other buy less and buy better? We can start by learning to share information on where to shop and which companies honor workers and natural habitats. As worshiping communities, we have to do a better job of reminding each other how shopping is of great religious significance.

Sabbath environmentalism is not limited to changed shopping patterns or practices. Our role as stewards or servants of creation is to actively seek to promote creation's ability to enjoy the *menuha* of God, and to enable creatures to attain their potential. In saying this, however, we need to be careful, for it would be a mistake to think that we can enable all of creation in this way. We simply do not understand fully how ecosystems work, and so we cannot possibly predict all the effects of even well-meant efforts. In our managerial zeal and desire to exercise a human influence, we frequently cause more harm than good. In fact, given our scientific and technological might and its often destructive effects, one of the most important things for us to do will be to pull back and minimize our direct influence on natural habitats. In pulling back we will give habitats and organisms the freedom and the space to be healed and restored. As we do this we will approach the Sabbath command to "provide for the redemption of the land" (Lev. 25:24).

Language of the land's "redemption" will sound a bit strange to our ears, because we readily assume that nature is amoral, without sin or fault, and thus not in need of redemption. But from a biblical point of view, and remembering that ungraced "nature" is not a biblical concept, we should understand that the land is a category thoroughly imbued by divine and human action. The land is what it is because of what God does through it and what we accomplish on it. It cannot be reduced to its materiality. This is why the ground, as Genesis 4:10 relates, can cry out to Cain in defense of Abel's shed blood. The land is in need of redemption because it is held captive by the bonds of human sinfulness and violence. The apostle Paul observes that creation waits "with eager longing" to be freed from the bondage of decay and that it groans with labor pains in eager expectation of the day of release, when it will enjoy the glory befitting children of God (Rom. 8:18–23). Creation is in this state of longing because it is currently disfigured by the effects of sin.

In this light it becomes easier for us to see that redemption of the land begins as we together with God undo the effects of sin. Practically speaking, this will involve the regular halting of human pressures and demands, a genuine Sabbath for the land. Lest we think this a fantasy, we should remember that in the past farmers would often let portions of their land lie fallow so that the pressures of crop production would be eased. More recently, land management bureaus of various state governments have implemented "rest rotational grazing" so that public lands are given a chance to recover from drought or overgrazing by livestock. Pastureland is given a full twelve months to rest and rejuvenate. Given that our forests, farmlands, coastlands, and oceans are currently being overtaxed by our unremitting extraction of timber, fiber, grains, and fish, would we not be modeling our Sabbath faith if we lobbied regulatory bodies to implement periods of rest, a sabbatical of sorts, in which the rhythms of creation could be restored and species be given the chance to replenish themselves? Clearly the length and time frame of such sabbaticals would vary from region to region and from ecosystem to ecosystem. But what would be gained is a recovery of the Sabbath year goal that all creation be given the opportunity to share in the rest of God.

Creation itself has something to teach us about rest. If we are attentive to the world, we will quickly see that Sabbaths are going on all around us. Various species of life demonstrate that rest is not an *option* for otherwise cutthroat biological processes but is in fact an inextricable part of the ways of life. We see this in plants and animals in states of dormancy and sleep and also in the witness of birds singing and wolves lounging or playing with cubs. Rest and celebration, even among wild organisms, promote healing, restoration, and reproduction. Sabbath rhythms are vital to the maintenance of all life. Humans are the unique species in that we have presumed to step outside of these created rhythms by working or shopping around the clock so that we can exalt ourselves. For the sake of our own health and the health of the creation, we need to implement creative ways to recover these rhythms.

Jesus, quite simply, asked us to "look at the birds of the air" and to "consider the lilies of the fields" (Matt. 6:26–28). Birds and lilies teach us that God provides with magnanimity and care. Seeing them we can know that God is with the whole creation, tending to its needs and making it a delight to the stomach, eyes, nose, ears, and touch. We need to cultivate a faith that affirms God's concern for us, but not only us, and thus let go of the anxiety and insecurity that propel us in the ways of ruthless exploitation and hoarding.

Biomimicry and ecodesign represent two promising developments that take seriously the great potential we have to learn from creation. In bio-mimicry engineers and scientists study closely the ways in which creatures interact in their environments to obtain or procure the goods, even medi-cines, they need. They try to figure out how sea abalones, without toxic waste or high-energy inputs, make polymer-type coatings that are stronger and tougher than anything we currently design. They observe blue mussels that make adhesives that set underwater and spiders whose fibers are much stronger and more resilient than what we now possess. By following their lead we can dramatically reduce our use of fossil fuels and our production of toxic residues. The assumption is that creatures can teach us in multiple ways to produce what we need in a manner that is cooperative rather than at violent odds with the habitats in which we live.[7]

Similarly, ecodesign aims to overturn the industrial way of making products. In the industrial method, whenever we make something we first extract a large amount of resources, apply lots of heat energy, and then after the product's limited use we are left with the problem of waste that is often toxic. Natural systems do not operate this way. Whatever is made does not end as unusable waste but as recyclable food or energy that can be used by somebody or something else. Ecodesign seeks to em-ploy sustainable methods of resource use and energy consumption in the manufacture of products ranging from shoes and carpets to buildings and cars, so as to end up with products that are not a toxic danger to humans or habitats. Ideally whatever products we make would have little to no harmful effect on the many members and memberships of creation.[8]

These two developments in design demonstrate that we can live in ways that are less destructive of our created home. As people committed to observing the Sabbath we need to take the lead in promoting practices that honor creation as the place where God's love is concretely realized and displayed. The Sabbath is not just for people. It is our responsibility not to unduly prevent creation's nonhuman members from enjoying their own forms of delight, from participating in the *menuha* of God. When we take up this responsibility, we will contribute to the healing of the earth.

12

Sabbath Worship

■ One of the great misconceptions about the Sabbath is that church membership exhausts our Sabbath responsibilities, that regular church attendance suffices to establish us as a Sabbath people. Actually we often, sometimes unwittingly, carry into our church life the anti-Sabbath expectations and dispositions—entertainment, anonymity, consumption, appearance, and self-exhibition—that now govern mainstream cultural life. Church, like everyplace else, can become a site of performance, exhaustion, and anxiety as we frantically perform all the tasks, ranging from numerous committee meetings to special programs, that don't fit anywhere else in our schedule. Not surprisingly, we then often do not enter the work week properly humbled, refreshed, and inspired by God's life-building ways. We have not shared in God's rest, love, and delight, because we have not really worshiped.

Another temptation, equally dangerous, is to think that worship is confined to one portion of one day. Worship is thus reduced to an item on a to-do list that we can check off. We do not enter into it with much thought or preparation, nor do we leave having been corrected or changed. For many of us, worship is simply too familiar. We have done it so many times and know exactly what to expect: three hymns or multiple praise choruses, a few prayers, an offering, a three-point sermon (hopefully not too long), and maybe the Eucharist. As a result, worship amounts to going through the motions. We are physically there but not really affected. We listen but do not really hear, observe but do not really see, give but do not really sacrifice, sing but do not really praise.

If we understood worship properly, we would quickly come to crave it as the high point of our life. For worship is the time when we most directly celebrate life's most profound meaning as a gift from God. It is where we acknowledge, examine, enjoy, and strengthen the realization that we all exist to be blessings to each other. Here we catch a better glimpse of God's ways and intentions as they are revealed in word and sacrament. In our worship we learn to cultivate (from the Latin word *cultus*, which, besides suggesting ritual and liturgy, refers to the patient, committed exercise of preparing a field or garden) our minds and hearts so that they more clearly see and respond to the grace of God at work all around us. We discover what is truly valuable in our workdays and activities, in our relationships and priorities, and what is not, and thus are positioned to shed those dispositions and habits that deny God's peace and joy and thwart our capacity to celebrate with each other the gifts of God.

One of the most serious, and finally destructive, habits we need to overcome is the near-natural propensity in us to worship an idol rather than God. Worship services may be constructed as grand (or not-so-grand) occasions in which we attempt to satisfy deep-seated fears and anxieties, needs and desires, by fabricating a god we can control or who will confirm (and be limited to) our expectations and wants. The problem with tame, comfortable gods of this sort is that they end up sanctioning precisely the frantic, vainglorious, and destructive priorities that lead to cultural and environmental ruin. "The search for God is not the search for comfort or tranquility, but for truth, for justice, faithfulness, integrity: these, as the prophets tirelessly reiterated, are the forms of God's appearance in the world."[1]

In joining worship to truth, we are compelled to attend to a fundamental concern: our naming of God and, by extension, our naming of our condition. Worship must be premised upon honesty. It must acknowledge that the God we worship forever exceeds what we might say or think and that the words we use to articulate God's love for us arise out of our confusion, pain, bewilderment, and hope. Even in our best worship we don't really comprehend what we are doing, because the divine love that calls us is unfathomable in its intimacy, depth, and breadth. Christian worship again and again calls our attention to the passion of Christ, so that in our dying and rising with him we can become new creatures (2 Cor. 5:17), witnesses to the peace, love, and delight that are the signs of God's own life.

Worship is entrance into our true humanity. Our common failure at worship reflects a profoundly disoriented life, an inability to examine carefully and honestly who and where we are. It suggests that we have not adequately grasped our situation in life as creatures made in the image of God, sharing our lives with other creatures, all dependent upon God and each other for our well-being. Indeed, the lack of authentic worship in our lives testifies to the practical absence of God, to the absence of a sense that God is the source, sustainer, and goal of all that we do and are. We don't really desire God, because what we need and want we can provide for ourselves. Since we are now, thanks to ever developing technologies and engineering innovations, masters of our own fate who can manipulate the world at will, if God appears at all it is as an ornament filling an emotional gap.

In this time of "practical atheism," when we worship with our lips but not in our practical living, the experience of authentic worship has become very difficult. We find it hard to move beyond our desire for control over the world to the lordship of Christ. If we are to recover the possibility of true worship, we will need to learn how to reconnect deeply with the grace of God at work around us, made manifest in the gifts of shared life and community. We need a refined capacity to see differently, in the light of Christ's crucifixion and resurrection.

We must learn to train our focus on life's interdependent goodness, potential, and joy, and also life's costliness, pain, and suffering, and then note God's involvement in the midst of it. Given the fast and superficial pace of our living, and our temptation to idolatry, this call to careful attention and appropriate naming of the meaning of things and events will not be easily carried out. But it is absolutely basic and necessary. Without it our worship, rather than being spontaneous and honest, will be forced and sentimental. We need the clarity of vision to perceive the loving, life-giving action of God at work in our midst. We need honesty and humility to acknowledge that without the gifts of God we are nothing.

Worship in Daily Life

Even the Roman Stoic philosopher Epictetus, a man not schooled in the Sabbath, understood that life is a gift: "I am a rational creature, and I ought to praise God: this is my work. I do it, nor will I desert this post, so long as I am allowed to keep it; and I exhort you to join in this same song." For Epictetus, praise is fundamental to a thoughtful and observant life: it alerts us to the fact that we are made capable of living only by the generosity of a divine being. The activity of praise is not abstract, optional, or merely ornamental. Nor is it appropriately limited to a few moments of the week. When we pay careful attention to the wide, enabling contexts of our living, it follows naturally. Thus it is our ongoing responsibility. So Epictetus continues: "Ought we not when we are digging and plowing and eating to sing this hymn to God: 'Great is God who gives us such implements with which we shall cultivate the earth. Great is God who has given us hands, the power of swallowing, a stomach, imperceptible growth, and the power of breathing while we sleep.' This is what we ought to sing on every occasion."[2]

That a philosopher not educated in God's drama of creation and redemption can see the need for praise and thanksgiving is striking. When we get to the most fundamental levels of human experience, we have to admit that we are helpless and utterly dependent on a power other than our own.

God's gifts are manifest everywhere we look: in the sun that daily warms us, the food that nourishes us, the water that slakes our thirst, plants that give us oxygen and flowers that offer fragrant beauty, sleep that rejuvenates us, the support and nurture of family and friendship. There is simply nothing too small or mundane to be an occasion for thanksgiving to God. Consider here the ancient Jewish morning prayer Asher Yatzar, which is offered in gratitude for a smoothly functioning digestive system:

> Blessed are You, HaShem, our G-d, King of the Universe, Who formed man with intelligence, and created within him many openings and many hollow spaces; it is revealed and known before the Seat of Your Honor, that if one of these would be opened or if one of these would be sealed it would be impossible to survive and to stand before You (even for one hour). Blessed are You, HaShem, Who heals all flesh and does wonders.[3]

Because there are no limits to the goodness of God, no detail that escapes God's notice or affirmation, there are no limits to the times and places wherein praise and worship to God are fitting. Paul's admonition to "rejoice always, pray without ceasing, give thanks in all circumstances" (1 Thess. 5:16–18) makes perfect sense to Sabbath people tuned to God's gracious presence in the world. When we punctuate key, though mundane, events in the day with praise, we consecrate our life and our living to God. We can sanctify our daily routines—when we rise and go to sleep, fill our car with fuel and our stomach with food, smell a flower or see a child smile—when we intersperse them with "Sabbath moments" of praise and thanksgiving.

Even if we could convert our entire personal existence into one unending act of praise, we could not completely name the depths of God's kindness. The hymn "The Love of God," written by Frederick Lehman, captures this awareness well, especially in the third verse—which draws upon the Jewish poem *Haddamut*, written in 1050 by Meir Ben Isaac Nehorai:

> Could we with ink the ocean fill,
> And were the skies of parchment made,
> Were every stalk on earth a quill,

And every man a scribe by trade
To write the love of God above,
Would drain the ocean dry.
Nor could the scroll contain the whole
Though stretched from sky to sky.[4]

The boundlessness of God's goodness and grace is our most basic starting point for worship. It is the root from which everything flows, the fact that establishes and makes possible every other fact. Even as we contemplate tragic dimensions of this life, their significance must ultimately, if not always clearly, be traced back to God's generative love.

If we are to be a Sabbath people, we need to figure out and practice the forms of worship that best reflect and respond to this grace of God. We need to develop the ways that will show forth the supreme worthiness of God, recognizing that in our acts of worship we give a most poignant expression to the practice of delight. As we proceed we will do well to follow the advice of Marva Dawn: "We need worship deep enough to change us, strong enough to kill our self-absorption, awe-full enough to shatter the little boxes into which we try to fit God, and thorough enough to address the world's needs because God is already at work to meet them."[5]

When we worship we make room for the presence of God to be seen, heard, tasted, touched, and felt in our midst. We allow God to change us individually and as communities so that together we better prefigure the kingdom of God. Worship is a very practical affair, because we cannot participate in God's kingdom if our relationships with each other are governed by jealousy, anger, pride, quarreling, and resentment. The apostle Paul says the kingdom of God is found in "righteousness and peace and joy in the Holy Spirit. . . . Let us then pursue what makes for peace and for mutual upbuilding" (Rom. 14:17, 19). The kingdom is a transformation of lives that is worked out daily in our speaking and our practical doing, resulting in relationships and communities that are healthy and whole.

John Howard Yoder has said: "The believing body of Christ is the world on the way to its renewal; the church is the part of the world that confesses the renewal to which the world is called. The believing body is the instrument of that renewal to the world."[6] As such, the church must be committed to the practices of reconciliation and forgiveness, the sharing of economic resources, the inclusion of all people in a transformed social body now under the lordship of Christ, and the mutually empowering disciplines of the Spirit. This is not an abstract calling. Paul frequently speaks about our potential wholeness using the metaphor of the body: we are all interdependent parts of one body needing each other and the direction of Jesus Christ. But Paul is also very clear that the worship performed by the body is not merely metaphorical: "Do you not know that your body is a temple of the Holy Spirit within you, which you have from God, and that you are not your own? For you were bought with a price; therefore glorify God *in your body*" (1 Cor. 6:19–20).

Paul's concern is not only that as communities we practice disciplines that will be conducive to harmony, peace, and joy (the social body) but that we also in the particularity and materiality of our hands and feet (the personal, physical body) engage in practices and habits that promote God's glory here and now. For many years spiritual concerns, often only vaguely articulated, have received the greater share of the church's attention. We speak frequently about, even if we do not always faithfully manifest, our need to be a unified and harmonious social body. But we have not sufficiently reflected on how our bodies can contribute to or detract from the glory of God and how individual bodies, when properly oriented to God, will inevitably contribute to the nurture and well-being of the social body. Thus as churches we tend to concern ourselves little about what we eat, how we dress, the places we shop, the kinds of homes we live in, the cars we drive, and the occupations we choose—as if these activities or habits were not occasions to honor God's grace and express our worship. We have divorced worship too much from our everyday lives and placed it in a purely spiritual realm, not realizing that in doing so we have rendered it abstract and anemic, cut off from the flows and patterns of daily life. Rather than having our worship grow seamlessly and spontaneously (more honestly?) from the activities we perform daily, we have confined it to special buildings and times that are susceptible to the fabrication and hype—the deceit of vainglorious and "empty words" (Eph. 5:6)—of the moment.

Weekdays, if they are to serve as good preparation for the Sabbath, must in some way be a participation in and manifestation of Sabbath goals. One of the first obstacles we must face is the frantic, harried schedules we—especially pastors—normally keep, which render us too exhausted and sleepy to worship on the Sabbath. Churches need to do a better job of instructing people in how we, as Dorothy Bass puts it, "receive the day."[7] Can we remove the clutter that does not serve a life-sustaining or life-promoting purpose? Can we calm the hurried pace that serves little more than to compensate for the insecurities we feel deep within us? One of the best sources of help would be to try to align our rhythm with a liturgical calendar, recognizing that there are seasons in life that include waiting, patience, confession, celebration, and hard work. Time is not an undifferentiated quantity. We need to perceive and engage it in more refined ways that honor it as a gift.

Saying no to time-wasting activities, however, will not be enough, for as we drop one unnecessary activity the space will get filled with another. A better approach is to learn to do essential tasks like house and yard work, food preparation, childrearing, and recreational activities in a Sabbath spirit and with an eye to their Sabbath potential. This will include doing tasks together with others rather than alone, because this will enable us to see more directly why we are doing them—to serve a common need and to be a benefit to each other as others have already benefited us—and how what we do is a source of common joy. We need the help and encouragement of each other to see how our daily mundane activities can be gateways into collective delight. Working together more will also add a festive and celebratory dimension to the tasks we perform.

If we are going to worship God through our bodies, we must learn to see our economic life and our daily work, our parenting and our household maintenance, our shopping and our recreating as occasions for the glorification of God rather than ourselves. It will require, much as the prophets and sages said, that we practice and celebrate our faith in the world and not simply through formal rites, since "the sacrifice of the wicked is an abomination to the LORD" (Prov. 15:8). It will also require us to rethink the nature of grace, seeing it less as a commodity (a special gift added to our own efforts) and more as God's active and abiding self-involvement in the world.

Responding to Grace

To speak about grace is to point to our being called to participate in God's own life and experience God's intense desire to love the world into being and to be ever present in it as its sustaining, vivifying life. The Hebrew word for grace, *hēn*, carries the connotation of a life-giving womb that nurtures, sustains, and protects. Grace is God's self-communication and self-dedication to us so that we might enjoy, already here and now, relationships that are informed by God's life-building ways. God is not far away from us, meeting us only at special times, but is as near to us as the movement of our own breath. The whole creation and we ourselves are expressions of this grace in its vitality and materiality. Grace is the communion of all life with God as the One who brings everything into existence and then sustains it daily. When we properly acknowledge this grace by our calling as creatures made in the image of God, we learn to promote God's life-giving intentions for the whole world. Just as the materiality of creation can be the expression of God's grace, so too can our bodies *in their materiality* be the visible (not merely audible) expression of worship. As a simple test, we might ask: how would we, *practically speaking*, praise God if we could not use words or pens?

One way to develop our worship is to pattern it on God's own praise as suggested by the first creation story. Genesis 1 describes in majestic fashion how God speaks light, sky, dry land and sea, vegetation and animal and human life into being. As the individuals and members of creation come to life, God pauses and sees that it is all very good. This creative work ends on the sixth day in God's own Sabbath worship on the seventh, but it follows seamlessly from and builds steadily upon the goodness that has emerged all along the way. We should pause to consider God's "seeing" the creation as very good, for, as Ellen Davis reminds us, biblical narrative rarely moves behind the action to reveal the moment of perception itself. Such moments are vital and terribly important, because they let us know that the perceiver has been moved and affected by a perception that will be of lasting importance and consequence.[8] God's worship, we can say, follows from the deep affirmation of the world in all of its primordial goodness. In creation's splendor, beauty, vitality, fecundity, and mystery God finds an occasion to pause, to celebrate, and to pronounce a grand "Amen"—let it be so!

Our perception, of course, is hardly as clear and honest as God's. We do not see with the love that God does, because our egos, and all the pride, jealousy, anxiety, arrogance, and insecurity they represent, get in the way of faithful seeing. This is why our worship, quite unlike God's, must always include time for repentance and forgiveness. We need to learn to see things and each other as the concrete expression of God's love rather than as occasions for the satisfaction of our desires, for when we do we will be led spontaneously to give praise and thanks to God for the integrity and splendor of creation, to share in the amen that marks all true worship.

Worship is our best and most focused response to the quality and goodness of creation all around us. Thus worship is less like work and more like play. The Catholic theologian Romano Guardini once said, "Worship has one thing in common with the play of the child and the life of art—it has no purpose, but is full of profound meaning. It is not work but play. To be at play, or to fashion a work of art in God's sight—not to create but to exist—such is the essence of the liturgy."[9] Or at least it has no purpose that we can devise and control. We play at worship as we fully immerse ourselves in and let our hearts be washed over by the life of God within and around us. We participate in the divine flow by submitting to its currents much as children submit to the flow of a game. We don't try to circumvent the game's order and cohesiveness by trying to impose our rules. Rather, we surrender ourselves so that we can more deeply appreciate and enjoy the to and fro of God's grace.

Our worship is good and true to the extent that we, like God, find creation delectable. To pronounce something delectable is to proclaim it a genuine delight, to find it especially pleasing or luscious, tasty, and delicious. Around our house nothing is more delectable than the fresh raspberries that grow in our garden. Come June we can hardly wait for the berries to get ripe. Our children fairly dance around the raspberry patch because they cannot contain their excitement at the prospect of enjoying this luscious fruit. The delight we share, however, is not simply in the taste, though this is a powerful attraction—store-bought berries are not nearly as good. What makes our berries especially delectable is that we have submitted our stories and schedules to theirs. Put simply, they have a hold on us. We share a history that extends beyond our eating to include the care of the raspberry patch, the pointing out of new shoots, the waiting and anticipation, the work of picking the berries while avoiding and enduring the plant's prickly barbs, and the yearly winnowing of dead stalks. Their delectability fuses with our work, our knowledge, and our enjoyment and thus contributes to a sense of intimacy. Things like raspberries become delectable when we perceive and know them in their rich depth and "from the inside."

This sense of intimacy mirrors, however imperfectly, the intimacy that sparked God's own delight following the perception of creation's goodness. God appreciates the goodness of everything because God sees and understands with unparalleled depth and clarity the love and joy that went into them. Though we are incapable of this divine appreciation ourselves, when we are at our creaturely best, we too will find the whole world tasty and a feast for the eyes and stomach. The root of the word *sapiential* (thoughtful, as when we are truly *Homo sapiens*) conveys at once knowing, seeing, and tasting. To be sapiential means to have entered into relationships with each other and with the world that are characterized by intimacy so close that the taste of (some, not all!) others—their unexpected sweetness, tangy zip, refreshing contentment, sometimes bitterness—remains in our mouth long after they are physically gone.

Worship and Service

Now we can better appreciate why the common meal or feast was and continues to be central to the worshiping community. Meals are the best practical context for building the intimacy and deep understanding that characterize the kingdom of God. When we eat together, we strengthen the physical and social body. When we celebrate the Lord's Supper, we infuse our eating and tasting, our knowledge and understanding, with the memory of Christ's life as the definitive pattern for authentic bodily upbuilding. The witness of Christ's passion, under the inspiration of the Holy Spirit, makes it possible for us to practice the sort of intimacy that will lead to genuine sharing, healing, forgiveness, celebration, and full-bodied delight. It would not be going too far to suggest that as we gather around the Lord's Table we proclaim, insofar as we are faithful, the delectability of creation. All our table fellowship, not only the eating done in church, ought to and can be a form of worship. Our eating together can become a demonstration of the intimacy and love that bind the whole creation together and make it such a delight. It can also be a regular practice in which the pain and suffering of creation can be honestly named and addressed.

I have often thought that too much of our worship focuses on the speaking of words. The sermon is given pride of place and time, even though it often contains a message we have heard several times before. Would we not do better to stress how the Word daily "becomes flesh" in our neighborhoods and communities, if from time to time we shifted the emphasis from podium speaking to face-to-face fellowship? Gathering around tables to eat, or in gardens to weed and harvest, or on building sites to do repair and construction—and not just on Sundays—we can learn more directly the ministry needs of the communities in which we move. Moreover, this face-to-face time can become the occasion for more exact and effective spiritual formation and mentoring.

One pastor I know of has baptismal candidates prepare for baptism by weeding a garden with a mentor. During this time of fellowship and service they discuss what discipleship, faithfulness, sin, and mercy are about. Another example is the regular table fellowship of coffee and cake practiced by the church I grew up in. This fellowship, punctuated by scripture reading and singing, strengthened and refreshed the community, allowing us to learn about and respond better to our personal and collective struggles and joys.

This more corporate sort of perception not only leads to authentic worship but quite naturally also leads to good work and good relationships. It will help us avoid what has become worship's great danger: blasphemy. Blasphemy has become a temptation to us precisely because we do not share the intimacy of relationships—with God, with each other, and with creation—that authentic worship presupposes. Our thinking, and thus also our speaking, has become hollow and readily deceiving because it is not firmly grounded in and informed by the particularities, limits, and potential of circumstance or the complexity of our life together. Because we are not faithful to and honest about our true condition—often because we do not see it with adequate patience and precision—a discrepancy between our words and our world readily develops. Though we may speak piously with our mouth, our bodily language, as reflected in our daily habits and dispositions, communicates the triumph of sin and thus renders our spoken words ornamental and false.

If we are to avoid blasphemy, we need to make our worship manifest and practical throughout the week. Not only will this bring our speech into greater alignment with our action, but our Sunday worship will become richer as it is tested, developed, and strengthened in the trials and opportunities of daily life. We will eat at the Lord's Table with greater honesty because we will have already welcomed each other at our tables at home and have sought reconciliation. We will give with greater conviction and understanding because we will have already sought to understand and attend to the needs of our communities and world, and more cheerfully as we have carefully noted and celebrated the many gifts that daily come our way. We will sing with greater exuberance and passion because we are testifying to the goodness of God revealed in our families, homes, gardens, friendships, workplaces, and neighborhoods.

Worship leaders and church services can go a long way toward helping us develop this embodied, continuous sort of worship. But to do this they must make it clear that worship, even though it requires and benefits from a formal time and focus, is not confined to Sunday mornings or particular buildings. We need instruction in the ways of grace and appropriate response, instruction that will help us to become more attentive to the work of God in our midst and more faithful to that divine work. We need communities that will nurture us in the arts of prayer, praise, and thanksgiving and that will encourage us to practice repentance, mercy, and forgiveness. This will not be easy, since we live in an idolatrous culture that is dramatically opposed to anything but self-worship and self-glorification, to anything that might call into question the supremacy of our own will and desire. Dawn says, "Worship ought to kill us." It needs to kill all vestiges of the ego that desperately wants to claim the world for itself, and it must make room for the inspiration of Christ to take root in our lives.

Fortunately, churches have long and varied traditions of formal and informal worship that can help us as we try to align our lives and stories with the life and intentions of God. Through good preaching and biblical instruction, we can become better informed about the grandeur and depth of God's great story of creation and redemption and then be inspired to participate more fully in this divine drama. Through our singing we can be exposed to the depths of human joy and pain and take comfort in the God who has "pitched a tent" among us and become our friend and Savior. In our prayers we can learn to identify and voice more precisely our true need and the many provisions God has to meet them, while through the sacraments we can witness and testify to the inspiring and correcting presence of God in the midst of our washing and eating, our marrying and dying. As we learn and are inspired, because of our worship, to see more clearly the grace of God active all around us, we will also learn to turn our bodies into gifts to each other and to God. Together we can create economies of gratitude and praise in which the blessings of God are fully celebrated and shared.

In a time of consumerist individualism, often empty of generosity and deep delight, we need practices that can lift us out of our narrowness and alienation. Sabbath worship can move us into nothing less than the love of God, a love that is stronger and more joyous than all our pain and suffering, more expansive and encompassing than our loneliness and fear, more life-giving than our sickness and death. Nothing, as Paul says, can separate us from the love of God. "For I am convinced that neither death, nor life, nor angels, nor rulers, nor things present, nor things to come, nor powers, nor height, nor depth, nor anything else in all creation, will be able to separate us from the love of God in Christ Jesus our Lord" (Rom. 8:38–39). What further reason do we need to worship God daily?

Notes

Chapter 1. Losing Our Way

1. Abraham Joshua Heschel, *The Sabbath: Its Meaning for Modern Man* (New York: Farrar, Straus and Giroux, 1951), p. 74.

2. Herbert McCabe, *God Matters* (New York: Continuum, 1987), pp. 85, 127. McCabe further notes that *grace* is the Latin form of "thank you," just as *eucharist* is its Greek form. To say thank you is thus to say something like "This gift makes me think of you," and so recalls our dependence on others and (finally) God.

3. For further information on our current food industry, see Andrew Kimball's *Fatal Harvest: The Tragedy of Industrial Agriculture* (Washington, DC: Island, 2002), Ken Midkiff's *The Meat You Eat: How Corporate Farming Has Endangered America's Food Supply* (New York: St. Martin's, 2004), and Eric Schlosser's *Fast Food Nation: The Dark Side of the All-American Meal* (Boston: Houghton Mifflin, 2001).

4. Ellen Davis, *Getting Involved with God: Rediscovering the Old Testament* (Boston: Cowley, 2001), p. 34.

Chapter 2. The Meaning of the Sabbath

1. Terence E. Fretheim, *God and World in the Old Testament: A Relational Theology of Creation* (Nashville: Abingdon, 2005), p. 50.

2. Richard H. Lowery, *Sabbath and Jubilee* (St. Louis: Chalice, 2000). He notes, "The *tôb* ['good'] refrain expresses God's intense pleasure at creation's every detail" (p. 86).

3. For an excellent treatment of *menuha* see Abraham Joshua Heschel's classic book *The Sabbath: Its Meaning for Modern Man* (New York: Farrar, Straus and Giroux, 1951), especially pp. 22-23.

4. Ibid., p. 89.

5. Ellen Davis, "Slaves or Sabbath-Keepers? A Biblical Perspective on Human Work," *Anglican Theological Review*, Winter 2001, p. 36. To say that we are to imitate God in our work does not mean that we can be perfect imitators or that we should follow all of God's ways (ways that sometimes employ immeasurable force—forest fires, earthquakes, volcanoes, floods, hurricanes—to accomplish a

beneficial outcome). Here we have to admit that we do not fully comprehend God's creative action and so must proceed with appropriate humility and prudence.

6. Lowery, *Sabbath and Jubilee*, p. 41.

Chapter 3. From Sabbath to Sunday

1. Jürgen Moltmann, *God in Creation: A New Theology of Creation and the Spirit of God* (Minneapolis: Fortress, 1993), p. 294.

2. As quoted in Pope John Paul II's May 31, 1998, apostolic letter *Dies Domini.* The entire text is readily available online at www.papalencyclicals.net/all.htm.

3. James Alison, *Raising Abel: The Recovery of the Eschatological Imagination* (New York: Crossroad, 1996), p. 55.

4. Both quotes come from Herbert McCabe's *God Matters* (New York: Continuum, 1987), pp. 97, 100.

5. John McDade, "Creation and Salvation: Green Faith and Christian Themes," *The Month* 23 (November 1990).

6. Alison, *Raising Abel*, p. 74.

7. My interpretation of the healing of the ten lepers in Luke 17 was greatly helped by Pastor Steven Yoder's sermon "Cleansed, Healed, Saved," given at First Mennonite Church in Bluffton, Ohio, on October 17, 2004.

8. McCabe, *God Matters*, p. 108.

9. Rowan Williams, *Resurrection: Interpreting the Easter Gospel* (Harrisburg, PA: Morehouse, 1982), p. 71.

Chapter 4. The Practice of Delight

1. Terence E. Fretheim, *God and World in the Old Testament: A Relational Theology of Creation* (Nashville: Abingdon, 2005), p. 23.

2. Thomas Traherne, *Centuries* 2.62, in *Poems, Centuries, and Three Thanksgivings*, edited by Anne Ridler (London: Oxford University Press, 1966).

3. David Bentley Hart, *The Beauty of the Infinite: The Aesthetics of Christian Truth* (Grand Rapids: Eerdmans, 2003), p. 253.

4. Josef Pieper, *In Tune with the World: A Theory of Festivity* (South Bend, IN: St. Augustine's, 1999), p. 23.

5. Ibid., p. 26.

6. Ibid., p. 28.

7. Michael Hanby, "The Culture of Death, the Ontology of Boredom, and the Resistance of Joy," *Communio* 31 (Summer 2004): 197.

Chapter 5. The Decline of Delight

1. Wendell Berry, *The Hidden Wound* (New York: North Point, 1989), p. 67.

2. Ibid., p. 65.

3. Michael Hanby, "The Culture of Death, the Ontology of Boredom, and the Resistance of Joy," *Communio* 31 (Summer 2004): 184–88.

4. Michel de Montaigne, "Of Coaches," in *Essays*, 3.6 (New York: Alfred A. Knopf, 1943).

5. Ivan Illich's reflections on health and embodiment can be found in *The Rivers North of the Future: The Testament of Ivan Illich as Told to David Cayley* (Toronto: House of Anansi, 2005).

6. This excerpt from the Nishmat prayer can be found in *The Book of Customs: A Complete Handbook for the Jewish Year*, compiled by Scott-Martin Kosofsky (San Francisco: Harper, 2004).

7. See Gary Cross's *An All-Consuming Century: Why Commercialism Won in Modern America* (New York: Columbia University Press, 2000) for a nuanced account of the many dimensions of twentieth-century consumerism.

8. Steven Best and Douglas Kellner, *The Postmodern Turn* (New York: The Guilford Press, 1997), p. 89.

Chapter 6. Pain and Suffering

1. As quoted by Susan Neiman in her book *Evil in Modern Thought: An Alternative History of Philosophy* (Princeton, NJ: Princeton University Press, 2002), p. 209.

2. Friedrich Nietzsche's critique of otherworldliness permeates many of his texts but is especially focused in *Twilight of the Idols*.

3. James Alison, *The Joy of Being Wrong: Original Sin through Easter Eyes* (New York: Crossroad, 1998), p. 165.

4. James Alison, *Raising Abel: The Recovery of the Eschatological Imagination* (New York: Crossroad, 1996), p. 60.

5. Stanley Hauerwas, *Naming the Silences: God, Medicine, and the Problem of Suffering* (Grand Rapids: Eerdmans, 1990), p. 83.

6. See Joel Shuman's account of the body of Christ as it relates to suffering in *The Body of Compassion: Ethics, Medicine, and the Church* (Boulder, CO: Westview, 1999), especially chapter 3.

7. See Stanley Hauerwas's essay "Should Suffering Be Eliminated? What the Retarded Have to Teach Us," in *Suffering Presence: Theological Reflections on Medicine, the Mentally Handicapped, and the Church* (Notre Dame, IN: University of Notre Dame Press, 1986), particularly pp. 175–79.

8. Frances Young's story is presented and analyzed by Samuel Wells in *Improvisation: The Drama of Christian Ethics* (Grand Rapids: Brazos, 2004). The quotation is from p. 179.

9. Ibid., p. 181.

10. Alison, *Raising Abel*, p. 172.

Chapter 7. Work and the Sabbath

1. Rowan Williams describes this well: "Divine creativity is not capable of imitation; it is uniquely itself, a creation from nothing that realizes not an immanent potential in the maker but a pure desire for life and joy in what is freely made" (*Grace and Necessity: Reflections on Art and Love* [London: Continuum, 2005], p. 164). The best that we can try to do is echo, not replicate, this divine, disinterested loving that is pure gift.

2. As quoted in Richard J. Clifford's "The Hebrew Scriptures and the Theology of Creation," *Theological Studies* 46 (1985): 522.

3. Wendell Berry, "Christianity and the Survival of Creation," in *The Art of the Commonplace: The Agrarian Essays of Wendell Berry*, edited by Norman Wirzba (Washington, DC: Counterpoint, 2002), p. 312.

4. The story about the Monhegan lobster fishers comes from Colin Woodard's essay "Lobster Stewards," *Orion*, November/December 2004, pp. 16–17.

5. Eric Gill, *A Holy Tradition of Working* (West Stockbridge, MA: Lindisfarne, 1983), pp. 63, 81.

6. Berry, "Christianity and the Survival of Creation," p. 312.

7. Eric Brende, *Better Off: Flipping the Switch on Technology* (New York: Harper, 2004), p. 31.

8. Donald Hall, *Life Work* (Boston: Beacon, 2003), p. 23.

9. Wendell Berry, *A Timbered Choir: The Sabbath Poems, 1979–1997* (Washington, DC: Counterpoint, 1998), p. 18.

Chapter 8. Sabbath at Home

1. As quoted by Vigen Guroian in "The Ecclesial Family: John Chrysostom on Parenthood and Children," in *The Child in Christian Thought*, edited by Marcia J. Bunge (Grand Rapids: Eerdmans, 2001), pp. 64–65.

2. Gaston Bachelard, *The Poetics of Space* (Boston: Beacon, 1969), p. 6.

3. Ibid., p. 7.

4. A handy discussion of the "new urbanism" as it relates to Christian themes can be found in Eric O. Jacobsen's *Sidewalks in the Kingdom: New Urbanism and the Christian Faith* (Grand Rapids: Brazos, 2003).

5. For an insightful critique of contemporary culture and a discussion of "focal practices," see Albert Borgmann's *Crossing the Postmodern Divide* (Chicago: University of Chicago Press, 1992).

6. As quoted in T. J. Gorringe's *A Theology of the Built Environment: Justice, Empowerment, Redemption* (Cambridge: Cambridge University Press, 2002), p. 197.

7. Christine Pohl, *Making Room: Recovering Hospitality as a Christian Tradition* (Grand Rapids: Eerdmans, 1999), p. 87.

Chapter 9. Sabbath Economics

1. Christopher J. H. Wright, *God's People in God's Land: Family, Land, and Property in the Old Testament* (Carlisle, UK: Paternoster, 1990), p. 117.

2. Richard H. Lowery, *Sabbath and Jubilee* (St. Louis: Chalice, 2000), p. 20.

3. Herman E. Daly, "Sustainable Economic Development: Definitions, Principles, Policies," in *The Essential Agrarian Reader: The Future of Culture, Community, and the Land*, edited by Norman Wirzba (Lexington: University Press of Kentucky, 2003), p. 64. See also Daly's *Beyond Growth: The Economics of Sustainable Development* (Boston: Beacon, 1996).

4. Wendell Berry, "Two Economies," in *The Art of the Commonplace: The Agrarian Essays of Wendell Berry*, edited by Norman Wirzba (Washington, DC: Counterpoint, 2002), p. 233.

5. Wendell Berry, "The Whole Horse," in *Art of the Commonplace*, p. 236.

6. See Thomas Frank's *One Market under God: Extreme Capitalism, Market Populism, and the End of Economic Democracy* (New York: Anchor, 2000).

7. For more information on local currencies and small-scale community development, see the resources of the E. F. Schumacher Society, www.schumach ersociety.org.

8. See www.hopecsa.org.

9. Wendell Berry, "The Idea of a Local Economy," in *Art of the Commonplace*, p. 260.

Chapter 10. Sabbath Education

1. Jane Jacobs, *Dark Age Ahead* (Toronto: Random House, 2004), p. 45.

2. Ibid., p. 62.

3. Robert Wilken, "Christian Formation in the Early Church," in *Educating People of Faith*, edited by John Van Engen (Grand Rapids: Eerdmans, 2004), p. 62. The quote from Augustine appears on the same page.

4. Eric Zencey, "The Rootless Professors," in *Rooted in the Land: Essays on Community and Place,* edited by William Vitek and Wes Jackson (New Haven, CT: Yale University Press, 1996), p. 16.

5. Susan Felch, "Doubt and the Hermeneutics of Delight," *Cresset*, Easter 2005, pp. 12–15.

6. Lowell Monke, "Charlotte's Webpage: Why Children Shouldn't Have the World at Their Fingertips," *Orion*, September/October 2005, pp. 29–30.

7. Simone Weil, *Waiting for God* (New York: Harper and Row, 1951), p. 112.

8. Simone Weil, *Gravity and Grace* (London: Routledge, 1963), p. 16.

9. Ibid., p. 27.

10. Ibid., p. 57.

Chapter 11. Sabbath Environmentalism

1. Nicholas Lash, *The Beginning and the End of "Religion"* (Cambridge: Cambridge University Press, 1996), p. 173.

2. The picture of a God who manipulates the world from beyond does not represent a biblical view. Terence Fretheim puts it this way: "God created a reliable and trustworthy world and, while God will be pervasively present, God lets the creation be what it was created to be, without micromanagement, tight control, or interference every time something goes wrong. . . . Not everything has been predetermined; genuine novelty is possible in God's world" (*God and World in the Old Testament: A Relational Theology of Creation* [Nashville: Abingdon, 2005], p. 7).

3. Wendell Berry, *The Unsettling of America* (San Francisco: Sierra Club Books, 1977), p. 110.

4. Ibid., p. 106.

5. Gerald Blidstein, "Man and Nature in the Sabbatical Year," in *Judaism and Environmental Ethics: A Reader*, edited by Martin Yaffe (Lanham, MD: Lexington, 2001), p. 140.

6. See the Worldwatch Institute's *State of the World 2004* (New York: W. W. Norton, 2004), pp. 86–87.

7. See Janine Benyus's *Biomimicry: Innovation Inspired by Nature* (New York: Morrow, 1997).

8. The main tenets of ecodesign can be usefully accessed in William McDonough and Michael Braungart's *Cradle to Cradle: Remaking the Way We Make Things* (New York: North Point, 2002).

Chapter 12. Sabbath Worship

1. Nicholas Lash, *The Beginning and the End of "Religion"* (Cambridge: Cambridge University Press, 1996), p. 179.

2. Quoted in Bernhard Lang's *Sacred Games: A History of Christian Worship* (New Haven, CT: Yale University Press, 1997), p. 13.

3. This prayer is readily available in prayer books and on the Web. See www.torahzone.com/AsherYatzar.htm.

4. The words and melody to the entire hymn can be found at www.cyberhymnal.org/htm/l/o/loveofgo.htm.

5. Marva Dawn, *Reaching Out without Dumbing Down: A Theology of Worship for the Turn-of-the-Century Culture* (Grand Rapids: Eerdmans, 1995), p. 126.

6. John Howard Yoder, *Body Politics: Five Practices of the Christian Community before the Watching World* (Scottsdale, PA: Herald, 1992), p. 78.

7. Dorothy Bass, *Receiving the Day: Christian Practices for Opening the Gift of Time* (San Francisco: Jossey-Bass, 2000).

8. From her essay "Seeing with God: Israel's Poem of Creation (Gen. 1:2-2:4a)," typescript.

9. Quoted in Lang's *Sacred Games*, p. ix.